HERBS
for Your Garden

Compiled from text by

Louise Egerton and Rolfe Bradley, F.R.H.S

Recipes by Janice Baker

BayBooks

An imprint of HarperCollins*Publishers*

A BAY BOOKS PUBLICATION
An imprint of HarperCollinsPublishers

First published as Growing Herbs *in 1981 and* Herbs for Better Living *in 1989*
This combined edition completely revised and updated in 1992

First published in Australia in 1992 by Bay Books, of
CollinsAngus&Robertson Publishers Pty Limited (ACN 009 913 517)
A division of HarperCollinsPublishers (Australia) Pty Limited
25-31 Ryde Road, Pymble NSW 2073, Australia

HarperCollinsPublishers (New Zealand) Limited
31 View Road, Glenfield, Auckland 10, New Zealand

HarperCollinsPublishers Limited
77-85 Fulham Palace Road, London W6 8JB, United Kingdom

Copyright © Bay Books 1992

National Library of Australia and
Cataloguing-in-Publication data:

Herbs for your garden.

   Includes index.
   ISBN 1 86378 028 9

   1. Herb gardening. 2. Cookery (Herbs). 3. Herbs – Utilisation.
   I. Egerton, Louise. II. Bradley, Rolfe. III. Baker, Janice.
   (Series: Bay Books gardening library).

   635.7

Cover photography by Lorna Rose
(Basket from Sherringhams Nursery, North Ryde;
herbs from Phillip Moore, Renaissance Herbs, Warnervale)

Photos by Lorna Rose on pages 6, 8, 10, 14, 15, 16–17, 27, 34, 40, 68, 74, 75
Photos by Denise Greig on pages 15, 38

Printed in Singapore

5 4 3 2 1
96 95 94 93 92

CONTENTS

GROWING HERBS

For thousands of years, herbs have been used as soothing balms, delicious teas, medicinal preparations, perfumes, dyes, wines, natural pesticides, cosmetic preparations, essential oils and vital recipe ingredients.

Nowadays you can experience the joy and delight of growing and using herbs whether you have room for a herb garden, or a pot on a sunny window sill.

Today, more than ever, the natural qualities of herbs are prized.

The recent resurgence of interest in growing herbs and using them in the home has many causes. The joy of cooking wholesome, tasty meals and the fun of creating new dishes from the cuisines of other cultures has encouraged using fresh and unfamiliar herbs — and spices.

In addition, a genuine concern about the environment and the possibly harmful side effects of some chemical products has created an enthusiasm for the natural — for herbal cosmetics, cleaning agents, fragrances, dyes, soaps and many more everyday household items.

Many of our popular herbs are easy to grow. Few are really difficult. Like all plants, however, they thrive if they are given the conditions that suit them. They are not plants which require any difficult or specialised treatment. This book stresses how to grow herbs so you can create a garden you will delight in that is filled with herbs you can use in cookery, for craft and many other purposes.

Traditional Herb Gardens

There are several traditional designs for formal herb gardens. The best known are the Knot, the Wheel, the Ladder and the Chequerboard.

THE KNOT GARDEN

A number of traditional shapes are used for growing beds of herbs but none is more intricate than the knot garden. As the name suggests, it consists of narrow, interlacing ribbon-like curves, each bed of herbs intersecting another bed of a different herb. Knot gardens were designed to be viewed from above, from the turrets, terraces or battlements of fine houses and castles. The work required to keep such a garden well-cared for today precludes many of us attempting this ambitious design but it is not really hard to do.

Right ◆ PATTERN FOR A KNOT GARDEN. CENTREPIECE COULD BE BAY TREE, A SPECIES ROSE OR CITRUS TREE. ROWS OF HERBS INTERTWINE AND ARE CLIPPED TO THE SAME HEIGHT AND SHAPE. HERBS COULD INCLUDE LAVENDER, THYME, SAGE, PARSLEY, VIOLETS, FENNEL AND CHIVES
Below ◆ FORMAL HERB GARDEN, WITH LAVENDER EDGED IN BOX

THE WHEEL

A well-loved shape is that of the wheel. Originally the different herbs were grown between the spokes of old cartwheels lain on their sides, the outer rim providing an edge. Today we can still grow our herbs in sections of a

circle but with paving bricks or stones for spokes, so we can wander into the middle of the 'wheel' and reach any herb we want. A bird bath, sundial or statue in the centre of this herb garden adds an element of tranquillity and old-fashioned charm to the garden. If there is room for a seat or bench, so much the better, for there will be a spot where you can soak up the peace and perfume of a timeless garden, away from the hurly-burly of twentieth-century life.

THE LADDER

The ladder is another formal shape often adopted for herb hardens. Herbs are grown in a rectangular bed with narrow footpaths along the sides and cutting across the bed to form 'rungs'. This bed shape is best suited to evergreen herbs that grow close to the ground.

CHEQUERBOARD

By missing out square pavers or bricks in a path and planting the square of soil with herbs, you can create a chequerboard effect. Variations on this pattern, with just the odd paver missing, provide less formal arrangement. Use only low-growing herbs. Mint is ideal, as the pavers restrict its rampant root growth.

HERB GARDEN INTERSECTED BY PATHS. SUGGESTED PLANTINGS ARE: 1 PURPLE BASIL, 2 THYME, 3 CHIVES, 4 DWARF ROSEMARY, 5 SAGE, 6 MINT IN SEPARATE BED, 7 PARSLEY, 8 MARJORAM, 9 SHALLOTS, 10 DILL, 11 GARLIC

Planning and Planting Your Herb Garden

There are a hundred and one ways to grow herbs — they are really very undemanding plants. Most need plenty of sun and well-drained soil. But you can grow some indoors, in pots or hanging baskets or massed together in different shaped containers on a patio or balcony.

They can flourish between pavers in the courtyard or peep from the brickwork of the barbecue area. Plant them in raised beds with the tallest growing erect and stately at the back or in the centre, and the smallest cascading down the sides. Some herbs make excellent border plants, while others that are tall and carry lovely flowers can be mixed in with border flowers or added to a cottage garden. Herbs were always an integral part of the traditional cottage garden.

Many aromatic herbs made good edging plants along pathways, their scent drifting up as you brush past them. Lavender and eau-de-cologne mint are good examples of this. Rockeries are another sheltered spot for many herbs,

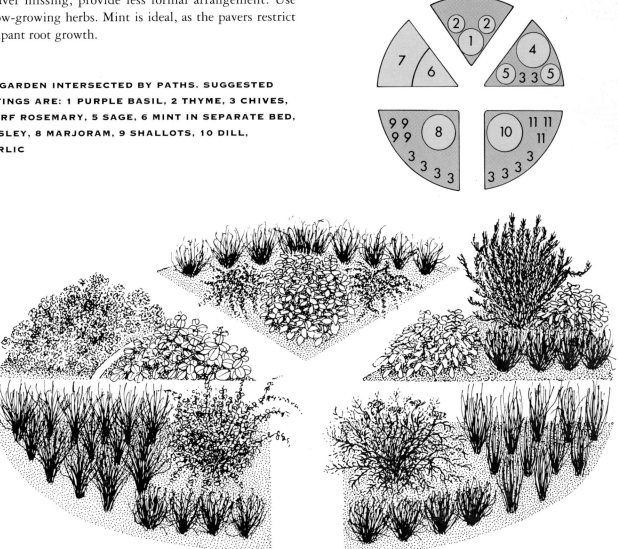

Right ◆ **THYME SEAT IN A HERB GARDEN**
Below ◆ **ALL SPECIES OF LAVENDER CAN BE HARVESTED AND DRIED EASILY**

though it is unwise to plant any that you cherish for their roots, as they are likely to be restricted in spread and hard to reach. If you have plenty of space you could design a formal herb garden based on traditional medieval or Elizabethan designs, which incorporated herbs grown for stewing and medicine as well as for flavour and perfume.

The important thing to remember is that your herbs must be accessible. When trekking out of your kitchen on a wet, dark night, you don't want to don a pair of wellies just to reach the parsley.

LIGHT

All herbs need light but while most herbs enjoy full sunlight, some need full shade, and others thrive satisfactorily under almost any light conditions.

Lack of early morning light can have a marked effect on growth and development. A plant given early light is faster in its development than a plant without it. Maximum height may occur as much as a month earlier with plants having morning light. The effect of aspect can be altered by buildings or other barriers. A garden may slope ideally to the north (in the southern hemisphere), and yet be without sun because of a high building or heavy shade trees.

WIND

Strong or persistent wind can be detrimental to many plants. Wind imposes stress on plants in many ways. On windy days, the soil tends to dry out much more quickly than in still weather. A combination of wind and heat is particularly damaging. Some herbs, especially some of the taller ones, have fairly brittle stems that are easily broken. For them a sheltered position is essential.

TEMPERATURE

Most plants have an optimum temperature at which growth is best. The most critical examples are those herbs that do not tolerate heavy frost and those that wilt in high temperatures. The latter usually need a shaded position and may be impossible to grow in areas where summer temperatures soar into the forties.

For frost susceptible plants, avoid a planting position just above a low fence or wall. Cold air rolls downhill and may be trapped by the wall and so form a frost-pocket as it is called. A frost-pocket may be some degrees colder than a higher part of the garden from which the cold air has escaped.

SOIL

Although there are many different types of soil the major types are clay soils, loams and sandy soils.

CLAY SOILS Clay soils are well known and sometimes disliked by the gardener because of the heavy, sticky nature of the soil when wet, and the way in which it hardens into cement-like blocks when dry. This makes clay soils hard to work. When wet the clods can't be broken and when hard and dry they tend to pulverise into fine dust if fractured.

Nevertheless, clay soils are easier to manager than sandy soils if you improve them properly, and provide drainage.

Building up clay soil entails adding generous quantities of organic matter and large quantities of sand. Once the latter is added no further sand will be needed. It can be forked into the top 10 to 20 cm at the rate of up to 5-10 m^3 per 100 m^2 of area, that is, a cubic metre of sand will dress 10 to 20 square metres of bed.

Clay soils are also improved by adding gypsum (calcium sulphate) or one of the proprietary improvers. If the area to be treated is not large, materials such as vermiculite and perlite can be used, but they are too expensive for treatment of large areas.

Organic matter doesn't last in the soil unfortunately because it is broken down by soil bacteria. This means that additional organic matter must be added to the beds, usually each season. During the dry season it can be left on the surface as a mulch and what remains forked in to the soil in autumn.

Suitable organic materials are cow manure, horse manure, sheep manure. Poultry manure is too strong to add in quantity but some can be mixed with animal manures, say, 1 part of poultry manure to 5 or 6 parts animal manure.

Properly made and well-ripened compost is excellent and can be used on all herbs, as can well decomposed leaf mould Other organic materials, such as those used for mulching, straw, sawdust, or grass clippings, should not be dug in around the herb plants, but can be left on the surface as a mulch.

The most useful characteristic of clay soil is that it tends to retain plant foods which would be quickly washed out of sandy soils by rain or watering. Clay soils also retain moisture well, in fact, they retain it too well and do not drain freely enough.

The two remedies available to improve drainage are subsoil drains and raised beds. The former are drains dug to a depth of 90 to 105 cm and spaced 9 to 15 m apart. Raised beds can be garden beds that are heaped up from 10 to 30 cm above normal soil level, or the soil can be retained above ground level in planter boxes or brick, concrete, railway sleepers or other suitable material. Sometimes both methods are combined, that is, subsoil drains are laid and beds raised above normal soil level.

SANDY SOILS Because sandy soils are easy to dig, gardeners sometimes prefer them to clay soils. Nevertheless, they are actually more difficult to manage. While clay soils retain moisture and plant food materials, sandy soils allow them to drain away into lower levels where plant roots cannot reach. The result is that more frequent watering and feeding are needed. Moreover, once a sandy soil dries out it can be most difficult to wet again.

In a clay soil, it is possible to add sand to improve the drainage and because the sand particles are relatively coarse they will be retained in the bed permanently. It is waste of effort to add clay to a sandy soil, because the extremely fine clay particles will soon be washed down into the lower soil levels, leaving the sand on top as before.

The only remedy is the regular and liberal addition of organic matter such as compost, animal manure, peatmoss, or a water-retaining inorganic material such as vermiculite. Because of cost, vermiculite could only be used in small beds or planter boxes.

LOAMS A loam is the ideal soil. It contains sand, silt and clay and can vary from a sandy loam to a clay loam. In these soils water-retention and plant food availability are good without the drainage problems of clays and sandy soils — the one too little, the other too much.

Soil improvement for a small herb garden is not too difficult a task. In the detailed herb list given in the next chapter the type of soil needed for each herb is given.

FEEDING

The lavish use of strong chemical fertilisers is not necessary for herbs but they can be fed in the ordinary way used for other plants. Some herbs do best in a richer soil than others and some grow well in almost any sort of reasonable soil.

Soils can have manures and compost added with advantage, and where food elements are deficient it may be necessary to supplement organic feeding with fertiliser dressing. But it is the organic matter that is essential. If properly prepared compost is available, fertilisers may not be needed at all, but this will depend in part on your soil.

As a general rule a lime or dolomite dressing will be needed where soils are naturally acid, as are most coastal soils. Ground limestone can be applied as in the table to raise the soil by 1 or 2 pH degrees.

	To raise 1 pH	To raise 2 pH
SANDY LOAM	225 g per m^2	450 g per m^2
LOAM	335 g per m^2	670 g per m^2
CLAY LOAM	395 g per m^2	790 g per m^2

The lime or dolomite can be applied before the first digging and then should be immediately forked thoroughly into the top 15 to 20 cm of the soil.

Most herbs like a soil pH around neutral point, pH 6.5 to 7.5, but recommended variations from this are given under each herb, where the most successful pH is known.

One week to ten days later the dressing of compost or manure can be worked into the soil. The quality added will depend on the plants to be grown. The herb notes in the next chapter will tell you which herbs like a rich soil with heavy dressings.

During plant growth, manure or fertiliser side dressings can be given if required. As always in the garden, the best rule is 'little and often'. Avoid heavy applications which can be harmful.

WATERING

Many herbs are shallow-rooted plants that will need more frequent watering than large shrubs and trees. Check dryness at least every second day in hot, windy weather. Mulches during summer help to save watering and keep soil cooler.

PRUNING

The most useful type of pruning for almost all herbs is tip-pruning. Pinch out the small tip shoot or bud, and this will encourage side growth and the development of compact bushy plants.

For herbs where the leaves are to be used — sage, thyme, marjoram, mint, parsley and so on — the picking of the leafy tips may be all the pruning needed. However, where there is insufficient picking, it may be necessary to pinch or clip plants to retain a compact shape.

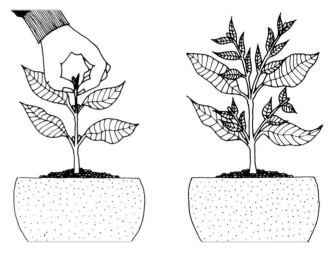

Left ◆ **TO PRUNE POT PLANTS, PINCH OUT THE TOP SETS OF LEAVES AND SHOOTS FROM LEAF AXILS**
Right ◆ **A COMPACT BUSHY SHAPE RESULTS**

Left ◆ **SOME HERBS ARE EASIER TO GROW FROM SEEDLINGS, AND ARE AVAILABLE FROM LOCAL NURSERIES, AND NURSERIES SPECIALISING IN HERBS**
Above ◆ **PACKETS OF HERB SEEDS**

Seeds or Seedlings?

Many herbs — such as basil, dill, nasturtium, parsley and chives — are easy to raise from seed, but they do need regular attention. You will have to wait at least six weeks and usually longer (up to a year for chives), before you can begin snipping them.

Some herbs are more trouble than others to grow from seed: parsley can take six weeks or more to germinate, French tarragon often doesn't set seed and is usually grown from cuttings, and others, like dill, dislike transplanting but can be sown direct into the garden and later thinned out.

The satisfaction is just as great if you opt to start with seedlings. When buying herbs in pots, always choose the most robust and sturdy plants. Containers planted with several types of herbs in the garden centre may look very pretty but if the herbs need different conditions, they won't look good for too long. It may be necessary to transplant each one according to its requirements when you get it home.

Raising Herbs from Seed

Sowing in seed trays is likely to be more successful than sowing directly into the open ground as conditions can be more easily controlled, particularly when sowing perennial herbs which are slower growing than annuals. Use punnets, small plastic pots, or ice cream and margarine containers with holes punched into the bottom, for drainage. Peat or fibre pots are biodegradable and can be planted out along with the seedling herb. Mix up a seed compost of one part peat, one part good quality sand loam and one part river sand, with a sprinkling of blood and bone; or buy a seed-raising compost.

Fill the containers to within 2 cm of the top of each rim. Snip one corner of the seed packet and open it carefully. Gently sprinkle a few seeds over the seed compost. Add a light sprinkling of compost over the top of the seeds, to about twice the seeds' depth. Firm down with a matchbox or flat board.

Place the containers in a sink of water, shallow enough to avoid water overflowing into the container but sufficient to seep into the soil through the drainage holes in the base of each container. When the top of the compost is damp, lift out the containers and drain. Stretch a piece of clear plastic wrap over each container. Leave trays in a sheltered, airy position, where you can keep an eye on them. Keep the mix moist and lift the plastic each night to discourage fungal problems.

Some seedlings may spring up in a week or so: others, like parsley, can take six weeks or more. Once you have shoots, remove the plastic entirely. When the seedlings have developed about four leaves and a small root system, it is time to transplant them from the seedbox into either the open ground or containers.

If you are transplanting into pots, fill the pot to within 2 cm of the rim with potting mix. Poke your finger into the mix and drop the seedling gently into the hole, ensuring no damage is done to the root. Press the mix gently around the seedling and top up with potting mix. Depending on the size of the pot, pop in as many seedlings as there will be room for fully grown plants. A pot of grown herbs should look filled and generous without being crowded.

To transplant into the open ground, the soil should be prepared. Gently lift out each seedling with the soil around its roots. Make a small hole in the ground, either with your finger or with a dibbler, just big enough to take the seedling. Pop it into the hole and press the surrounding soil firmly but gently around the seedling. Do likewise with the other seedlings, leaving enough space for each plant to grow to its full potential. Water the new seedlings in, to settle the soil around them and encourage root growth.

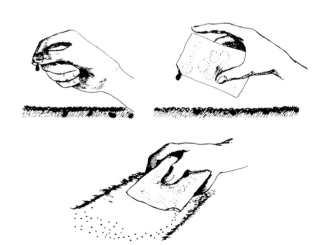

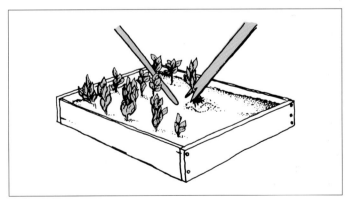

Above ♦ **TRANSPLANT WHEN THE SECOND PAIR OF TRUE LEAVES HAS DEVELOPED**

Left ♦ **SNIP PACKET, SPRINKLE SEEDS OVER COMPOST**

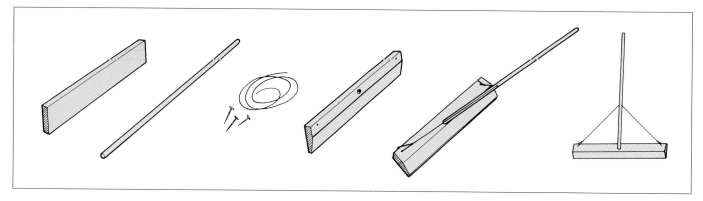

MAKE A SIMPLE SPREADER AT HOME, TO PRODUCE LEVEL SOIL AND SPREAD FERTILISER EVENLY

Preparing a Seed Bed

Seeds can be sown directly from the seed packet, taking care to space out seeds. Small seeds can be shaken out to ensure even distribution. Large seeds can be tapped individually into the soil directly from the packets.

To produce level soil or spread fertiliser evenly, make a simple spreader at home. Use a piece of hardwood about 1000 mm long x 100 mm x 25 mm, a rake handle, some wire and nails. Plant off one edge of the hardwood. Bore a hole halfway through to take the wire. Nail the handle in place on the leveller-head. Guy it by threading wire through the holes to the handle.

Planting out Potted Herbs

If you plan to plant out your herbs, prepare the bed first and water the plant some hours before transplanting. With the fingers of one hand gently gripping the main stems of the herb, invert the pot and tap it firmly on the bottom and against the sides. The entire herb and root ball should drop out in one piece. If you have difficulty in dislodging it, then soak the plant in warm water for a few minutes and drain, before trying again.

Dig a suitable-sized hole for the herb with a trowel. Gently straighten out any curling roots, loosen the earth from around root tips, taking care not to damage any, then place the root ball into the hole. Position it correctly, make sure it isn't leaning over and is planted at the exact height it was planted in the pot. Very often the plant looks more attractive from one angle rather than another, so experiment a little. Once in position, fill in the hole with soil all around. Firm in the plant and give it a good drink. Keep an eye on it for the next few days, making sure it does not lack water, and mulch around the herbs before hot weather arrives.

Right ◆ **THIS ROSEMARY CUTTING HAS A GOOD ROOT SYSTEM**
Far Right ◆ **PENNYROYAL BEING PREPARED FOR ROOT DIVISION**

Propagation

The best time for dividing perennials is in autumn and winter, though early spring is also possible. Woody-stemmed herbs can be propagated from softwood cuttings in early summer.

LAYERING

Use scented geranium, lemon balm, all mints, white horehound, marjoram, hyssop, rosemary (slow), sage, savory and thymes. Plants often propagate themselves by layering. One stem of the plant straying across the soil often starts to put down roots in a certain spot. Encourage this by taking one or two stems and gently securing them to the ground with a hairpin or some U-shaped piece of wire. Water this spot liberally and eventually the plant will put down roots. About six weeks after it has rooted, you can cut the connecting stem and move the plant elsewhere.

CUTTINGS

Most herbs can be propagated from cuttings except those that grow in clumps e.g. dandelion, borage, comfrey, lemon grass and horseradish, but this method is most useful with woody-stemmed herbs.

Cuttings are best taken after flowering. Take stems that are firm and healthy, with a woody heel if possible, and trim off the bottom leaves. Put the cuttings in a seed-raising mix and water them well. Dipping the bases in hormone rooting powder will help. Check the date on the powder as it is only effective for a certain time. Spray the leaves regularly with water and never allow the soil to completely dry out.

To maintain the moisture in the soul, you can cover the container of cuttings with transparent plastic, glass or cling wrap but air cuttings at least every 24 hours. Leave the cuttings in a sheltered warm spot out of direct sunlight.

When cuttings show new growth, you know they have rooted successfully. Wait a further two weeks or so before transplanting cuttings into containers or open ground. Softwood cuttings usually take a few weeks to strike; hardwood cuttings can take as long as six months.

ROOT DIVISION

This is an easy way of multiplying your stock of perennial herbs, provided you have a healthy, well-rooted plant in the first place. Dig up your existing plant or turn it out of its pot. Remove surrounding soil and cut or pull the root apart. Repot or replant each section as a separate plant. Do this early in the growing season, as new growth is beginning. It is not always necessary to dig up the entire plant. If dividing strongly growing plants in summer or autumn, you may need to trim foliage to compensate for root interference.

Left ◆ THE CORRECT WAY TO TAKE A CUTTING
Below ◆ TO POT CUTTINGS, DIBBLE A HOLE IN PREPARED POTTING MIX, AND INSERT THE CUTTING, FIRMING THE SOIL AROUND TO STAND THE CUTTING UPRIGHT

Companion Planting

By growing specific herbs and other plants together, it has been found that the association can be mutually beneficial.

Companion planting, or allelopathy as it is scientifcally known, is both an art and a science. To know which plants are happiest growing together we have compiled a chart. Many of these discoveries have been stumbled upon by gardeners and passed on by word of mouth. Some strange bedfellows remain scientifically unexplained and yet they seem to work. You may dicover new successful partnerships yourself.

Try planting a few herbs near a group of companion plants; e.g. three basil plants could be planted beside or within a bed of asparagus or tomatoes.

You can also use a variety of herbs as attractive and beneficial edging or border plants; e.g. a bed of cabbage could be edged with oregano, dill, chamomile, coriander, mint, rosemary, sage and thyme. Variety can help to reduce pests and diseases.

**COMFREY IN AN URN
(SYMPHYTUM OFFICINALE)**

HERBS	GOOD COMPANIONS	BAD COMPANIONS
Anise	coriander	—
Basil	tomatoes, asparagus	rue
Bee balm	tomatoes	—
Borage	strawberries, tomatoes, squash	—
Caraway	peas	fennel
Chamomile	onions, cabbage, broccoli, peppermint	—
Chervil	carrots, radishes, dill	—
Chives	carrots, apple and other fruit trees, roses, parsley	—
Comfrey	most vegetable crops	—
Coriander	carrots, cabbage, anise	fennel
Dandelion	fruit trees	—
Dill	cabbage, corn, lettuce, cucumber, broccoli, onions, carrots	fennel
Fennel	—	beans, caraway, dill, tomatoes, kohlrabi, wormwood
Foxgloves	improve storage quality of potatoes, tomatoes and apples	—
Garlic	roses, fruit trees, raspberries, tomatoes	peas, beans, cabbage, strawberries
Horseradish	potatoes, fruit trees	—
Hyssop	grapes, cabbage, Brussels sprouts, most vegetable crops	radishes
Lemon balm	tomatoes, most vegetable crops	—
Lovage	vegetable crops	—
Marigolds	French beans, potatoes, corn, tomatoes, fruit trees	—
Marjoram	vegetable crops	—

HERBS	GOOD COMPANIONS	BAD COMPANIONS
Mint	cabbage family, tomatoes	parsley
Nasturtium	radishes, potatoes, fruit trees, broccoli, cabbage, squash, pumpkin, tomatoes, cucumber	—
Oregano ✓	broccoli, cabbage, cauliflower, cucumber, grapes	—
Parsley ✓	beans, chives, roses, tomatoes, asparagus, carrots, turnips	mint
Pennyroyal	broccoli, Brussels sprouts, cabbage	—
Peppermint	cabbage, chamomile	—
Pyrethrum	strawberries	—
Rosemary ✓	sage, carrots, cabbage family, beans	potatoes, rue
Rue	fig trees, roses, other shrubs and trees	sage, basil, rosemary
Sage ✓	rosemary, cabbage family, carrots, peas, beans	rue, cucumber
Salad burnet	thyme, mint	—
Savory, summer	onions, beans	—
Southernwood	cabbages, fruit trees	—
Stinging nettles	currant bushes, soft fruits, tomatoes, most herbs	—
Tansy	fruit trees, roses, cabbage family, raspberries, blackberries, most soft fruits, grapes	—
Tarragon	all-purpose garden helper	—
Thyme ✓	cabbage	—
Valerian	vegetable crops	—
Yarrow	vegetable and herb crops	—

From Top ◆ LEMON BALM (*MELISSA OFFICINALIS*), ROSEMARY IN FLOWER (*ROSMARINUS OFFICINALIS*), TANSY (*TANECETUM VULGARE*)

Container Clues

Anyone with a balcony, courtyard or small backyard can grow a splendid array of herbs in a comparatively small space by using a variety of containers. If you want to grow some of the deeply rooted herbs, however, like horseradish, you will have to build a raised bed or find an extremely deep pot. Very tall herbs, like lovage, are not really suitable for pots.

Window boxes, hanging baskets, urns, pots or old sinks can all be made suitable homes for herbs and there are a

Below ◆ **STRAW-BERRY POT OF HERBS, BASIL, PARSLEY, FEVERFEW AND TANSY**

number of proprietary potting mixes that provide adequate soil — though some may not be very nutritious for any length of time. For this reason you may wish to mix your own. Remember, containers are very prone to drying out in the midday sun and this can be fatal for small herbs. Peat, once dried out, is difficult to moisten again, so use a mix of four parts crumbly, top-quality loam, two parts moist peatmoss and compost and two parts coarse river sand. The mix will be rather heavy, so if you intend to move the pots around the garden, choose smallish ones and don't use large hanging baskets as their weight, when wet, may strain their fastenings.

Raise containers on tricks or supports that will provide good air circulation around the pot. Watch your herb

very carefully through the hot summer months to make sure they don't dry out. Test with a finger 2.5 cm into the potting mix and if it feels dry, the plants need watering — this may be necessary twice a day in summer.

Hanging baskets are particularly prone to drying out and are easily forgotten. Always line the basket with sphagnum moss, plastic, bark, or special fibre available from garden centres. This will help the soil from drying out quite so quickly.

Unlike herbs in well-prepared open ground, herbs in containers do need feeding. During the growing season liquid feed plants every two weeks. Nothing is required in winter.

REPOTTING

The best time for most herbs to be repotted is spring. Some can be potted up in autumn and rest quite contentedly through to the next spring when they will burst into life.

Wash pots in warm, soapy water or disinfectant with a wire brush before use. This ensures the pot is not holding any damaging microbes or spores.

To prevent clogging over the pot's drainage holes, cover them with broken clay pot pieces (crocks) or gravel. Add a little potting mix before tapping out the herb from its previous pot. If the plant is root-bound and won't budge, sink the pot in warm water for a couple of minutes.

To tap out the plant, place two fingers of one hand around the stem of the plant, then carefully invert the pot and gently tap its bottom and sides with your other hand. The plant should slip out complete with soil ball. If possible, gently tease out the root tips but do not damage them.

Sit the plant on the fresh potting mix in the new pot and add as much mix as you need to raise the plant to within 2 cm of the pot rim. Then fill in the edges around the plant, firm down and add any extra mix to make level. Give the herb a long drink. Place it in a shady place for a couple of days to let it acclimatise, then move it into the sun (unless it is a shade-lover).

STRAWBERRY POTS

Herbs tumbling out of the pocket openings of these terracotta urns look lovely but the secret to their success lies in the types of herbs used and the method of planting. In the top, most low or medium height herbs can be planted, but in the pockets you will need a bushy creeping plant and probably the most suitable is thyme.

The way to plant is to fill the pot as you would any other, up to the first pocket. Sink the roots of the first thyme plant into the soil from the inside and poke only the leaves out of the pocket. Firm down the roots in the soil. Then fill up the urn with potting mix to the next pocket and repeat the process. Continue until you reach the top. If you fill up the urn first and insert the plants into the pockets from the outside, you will find they may be dislodged during the first good watering. Water slowly, making sure the water penetrates the potting mix, and does not just run out of the pockets.

Above ◆ **AN ENTIRE HERB GARDEN CAN BE GROWN IN POTS — EVEN QUITE LARGE PLANTS, LIKE THE LAVENDERS, WILL THRIVE**

Left ◆ **HERBS IN A STRAWBERRY POT — CHIVES, PARSLEY AND SAGE**

Herbs for Special Purposes

These lists will help you to choose herbs that enhance the landscape and suit the climatic conditions of your garden.

HERBS FOR SHADE AND FILTERED SUNLIGHT

Angelica
Balm
Basil
Bergamot
Chervil
Cicely
Costmary
Cress
Elecampane
Golden elderberry
Lovage
Mint
Tansy
Tarragon
Turmeric
Vanilla
Violet
Woodruff

HERBS FOR GARDEN FRAGRANCE

Ambrosia
Costmary
Lavender
Lemon verbena
Mints
Pelargonium
Rosemary
Tansy
Thyme
Violet
Woodruff

HERBS FOR CARPETING

Chamomile
Dwarf savory
Low-growing mints
Prostrate rosemary
Thyme
Woodruff

HERBS WITH GREY LEAVES

Catmint
Catnip
Horehound
Lavender
Sage
Southernwood
Wormwood

HERBS FOR INFORMAL EDGING AND HEDGING

Chives
Lavender
Pelargonium
Rosemary
Violet
Wormwood

HERBS FOR MOIST SOILS

Angelica
Balm
Bedstraw
Bergamot
Black mustard
Comfrey
Elderberry
Elecampane
Garlic
Horseradish
Lovage
Pennyroyal
Pepper
Peppermint
Sage
Sorrel
Summer savory
Vanilla
Violet
Woodruff

HERBS FOR FERTILE SOILS

Angelica
Arrowroot
Balm
Basil
Bay
Bergamot
Cardamom
Chamomile (Roman)
Chives
Cicely
Comfrey
Corn salad
Costmary
Cumin
Dandelion
Fennel
Foxglove
Ginger
Horehound
Horseradish
Lovage
Marjoram
Mint
Onion
Parsley
Pepper
Peppermint
Sage
Sorrel
Spring onion
Summer savory
Turmeric
Violet
Woodruff
Zedoary

HERBS FOR COOL CLIMATES ONLY

Chervil (sow seeds in autumn only in warmer areas)
Cicely
Corn salad

HERBS FOR THE BATH

Use essential oils from these herbs to:

◆ RELIEVE ACHING MUSCLES

Lavender
Rosemary
Thyme

◆ HELP YOU RELAX AND SLEEP

Bergamot
Chamomile
Geranium
Lavender
Lemon balm
Lemon grass
Marjoram

HERBS FOR A TEA GARDEN

Chamomile (German and Roman)
Catnip
Chicory
Dandelion
Lemon balm
Lemon grass
Lemon verbena
Mint (peppermint and spearmint)
Sage

HERBS CAN BE DECORATIVE AND ALSO HAVE MANY USES

Herb Calendar

COMMON NAME	SYNONYMS	BOTANICAL NAME
Basil	includes sweet basil; bush basil	Ocymum basilicum O. minimum
Bay	Grecian, Roman, noble or royal laurel, sweet bay	Laurus nobilis
Bergamot	bee balm, Oswego tea	Monarda didyma
Caraway	—	Carum carvi
Catmint	catnip, catnep, field balm	Nepeta cataria
Chamomile	Roman, garden or low chamomile; German or wild chamomile	Matricaria chamomilla Anthemis nobilis
Chervil	French parsley, salad chervil	Anthriscus cerefolium
Chicory	wild chicory, succory, wild succory	Cichorium intybus
Chives	includes garlic and onion chives	Allium schoenoprasum
Coriander	Chinese parsley, cilantro	Coriandrum sativum
Dill	dilly, garden dill	Anethum graveolens
Fennel	common or wild fennel	Foeniculum vulgare
Garlic	—	Allium sativum
Geraniums, scented	includes rose; peppermint; coconut; lemon	Pelargonium graveolens P. tomentosum P. enossularoides P. limonium
Ginger	African or black ginger	Zingiber officinale
Horseradish	—	Cochlearia armoracia

GROWTH HABITS	PROPAGATION
annual 15 to 60 cm, small white flowers and shiny oval leaves, full sun or semi-shade, moist rich soil	seeds direct late spring or early summer, 15 to 30 cm apart
evergreen tree to 11 m, white flowers and purple-black fruits, full sun or semi-shade, moist well-drained soil	very slow growing; plant well-established tree in pot or ground
perennial to 1.2 m, attractive lavender, pink or scarlet flowers, morning sun or semi-shade, moist rich soil	root divisions any time of year or seeds in spring, 15 cm apart
biennial to 60 cm, fine lacy leaves and umbrella-like clusters of white flowers, full sun, well-drained soil	seeds direct spring or autumn, 20 cm apart, thin out
perennial to 1.6 m, pointed scalloped leaves and white flowers with purple spots, full sun or semi-shade, well-drained soil	seeds, cuttings or root divisions in spring, summer or autumn respectively
perennial to 30 cm, white or yellow flowers, full sun, any soil; annual to 45 cm, similar flowers to Roman chamomile, full sun, any soil	tip cuttings any time of year, seeds or root division
annual to 50 cm, finely cut leaves like parsley and clusters of white flowers, semi-shade, moist rich soil	seeds direct spring or autumn, 10 cm apart
perennial to 1.5 m, blue or violet flowers, full sun, rich soil	seeds direct in spring, 45 cm apart
perennial to 20 cm, long thin strap-like leaves and purple flowers, moist rich soil, sun or semi-shade	seeds direct or plant bulb divisions, spring, summer or autumn, 20 cm apart
annual to 60 cm, parsley-like leaves and pink-white flowers, full sun, light soil, protect from winds	seeds direct spring or early summer, 30 cm apart, thin out
annual to 90 cm, fern-like leaves and attractive yellow flowers, full sun, well-drained rich soil	seeds direct spring, summer or autumn, in clumps, 30 cm apart
perennial to 1.5 m, feathery leaves and yellow flowers, full sun, rich well-drained soil, protect from winds	seeds direct late spring or early summer, 20 cm apart, thin out
perennial to 1 m, flat strap-like leaves and mauve-white flowers, full sun, well-drained rich soil	bulbs in spring or autumn, 25 mm deep, 15 cm apart
perennial to 1 m, large frilled leaves, pink flowers trailing perennial to 30 cm, small white flowers perennial to 30 cm, small pink flowers perennial to 1.5 m, small white flowers all require full sun or semi-shade, well-drained soil	root or tip cuttings in late summer
perennial to 1.5 m, spikes of white and purple flowers, semi-shade, well-drained soil with lime	root pieces in late spring, 3 cm below surface
perennial to 1 m, rosettes of dark green leaves like spinach and tiny white flowers, semi-shade, moist rich soil	root pieces 15 cm long, plant horizontally 30 cm apart, cover with 5 cm soil, roots harvested 6 to 7 months later

COMMON NAME	SYNONYMS	BOTANICAL NAME
Lavender	Includes English; French; Italian/Spanish	*Lavandula vera, L. officinalis or L. spica* *L. dentata* *L. stoechas*
Lemon grass	—	*Cymbopogon citratus*
Lovage	European lovage, lavose, sea parsley	*Levisticum officinale*
Marjoram	includes garden, knotted, and sweet marjoram	*Origanum majorana*
Mint	includes common mint (spearmint); applemint; peppermint; pennyroyal	*Mentha spicata* *M. rotundifolia or M. suaveolens* *M. piperita* *M. pulegium*
Oregano	wild marjoram	*Origanum vulgare*
Parsley	includes Hamburg, Italian (flat-leaved) and curly-leaved (common or garden) parsley	*Petroselinum crispum*
Rosemary	includes ordinary rosemary and prostrate rosemary	*Rosmarinus officinalis*
Sage	garden sage	*Salvia officinalis*
Savoury	includes summer savoury; winter savoury	*Satureia hortensis S. montana*
Sorrel	common, garden or meadow sorrel, sourgrass	*Rumex acetosa*
Tarragon	estragon, includes Russian and French	*Artemisia dracunculus*
Thyme	includes common or garden thyme, lemon thyme	*Thymus vulgaris T. citriodorus*

GROWTH HABITS	PROPAGATION
perennial to 1 m, silvery grey leaves and classic spikes of blue-purple flowers perennial to 1 m, small lavender flowers perennial to 30 cm, deep purple flowers, many varieties of lavender available, with white, pink, green, blue, and purple flowers, full sun, rich well-drained soil	seeds in punnets or cuttings, spring or autumn
perennial to 2 m, long slender leaves, full sun, rich soil	plant division
perennial to 2 m, dark green celery-like leaves and white or yellow flowers, sun or semi-shade, moist rich soil, protect from winds	seeds direct spring or autumn, 60 cm apart
perennial 25 to 75 cm, small oval leaves and white or purple flowers, full sun light, well-drained soil	seeds, cuttings and root divisions late spring or early summer, 30 cm apart
perennial to 60 cm, white flowers perennial to 1.5 m, mauve flowers perennial to 90 cm, pinky mauve flowers perennial to 15 cm, mauve flowers all the mints prefer semi-shade, but some will grow in sun, moist rich soil	root divisions, cuttings and seeds any time of year, best in large pots to contain spreading roots
perennial to 75 cm, tiny purple flowers, parent plant of marjoram, similar growth habits	seeds, cuttings and root divisions late spring or early summer, 30 cm apart
biennial 15 to 60 cm, flat or curly leaves and yellow flowers, full sun or shade, moist well-drained soil semi-shade, but some will grow in sun, moist rich soil	seeds direct in spring, summer or autumn, 20 cm apart
evergreen perennial 20 to 150 cm, grey-green narrow leaves and attractive blue flowers, full sun or semi-shade, rich well-drained soil	seeds or cuttings in spring, summer or autumn, 100 cm apart
perennial to 60 cm, grey-green leaves and purple flowers, full sun, alkaline soil	seeds or cuttings in late summer or autumn, 30 cm apart
annual to 60 cm, bronze-green leaves and pink flowers, full sun, light soil; perennial to 40 cm, semi-prostrate rounded leaves and white or lavender flowers, full sun, light soil	seeds direct in spring and summer, 15 cm apart; seeds or cuttings in autumn, 30 cm apart
perennial to 90 cm, big flat heart-shaped leaves, full sun, moist rich soil	seeds direct or root division in spring or autumn, 15 cm apart, divide established plants
perennial to 1 m, Russian — rough light green leaves, French — dark slender leaves, small white or yellow flowers, full sun, light well-drained soil, protect from winds	cuttings or seeds in spring or summer, 60 cm apart
perennial to 30 cm, pretty white, pink or purple flowers; perennial to 30 cm, tiny white flowers, silver and gold leaved varieties available, need full sun, well-drained soil	seeds, cuttings, root divisions in spring or autumn, 15 cm apart

GROWING EACH HERB
Growing Guide A to Z

Herbs with their many culinary, cosmetic and medicinal uses have become very popular. Grow them at home and have a readily-accessible and fresh supply on hand whenever required. It is as satisfactory to use home-grown herbs as it is to use home-grown vegetables. Quality and freshness is assured.

Most herbs are not difficult to grow and most do not take up a great deal of space. They are not plants which require any difficult or specialised treatment. For each herb listed here, are guidelines for the most favourable soil, water, light and heat conditions.

What exactly is a herb? Botanically, a herb is any small plant that is not strongly woody and is annual, biennial or perennial. This book will regard as herbs, those plants that are mostly low-growing and whose parts — leaves, seeds, flowers, bark, stem or roots — are used for flavouring food or in cosmetics or medicine.

Some herbs are used more frequently than others in the kitchen. Recipes for interesting dishes have been included for the more popular herbs.

Agrimony

AGRIMONIA EUPATORIA, COCKLEBURR, STICKLEWORT

This is an upright, tall growing, perennial herb 60 to 150 cm high, with variable pinnate leaves measuring 20 cm long at the base to 8 cm long at the top. The lower leaves have more leaflets than the top leaves. The small, star-like, yellow flowers occur in slender, tapering spikes. The plant is green, aromatic, and has silky hairs beneath leaves.

Agrimony has been used medicinally and for a herbal tea. It is the source of a golden yellow dye.

GROWING Agrimony will grow anywhere except in deep shade, and in any average soil providing it is well-drained. Plants are frost tolerant.

Propagate plants by seed or division of the roots.

Allspice

PIMENTA DIOICA

Belongs to a genus of aromatic trees, native to tropical America and the West Indies. This tree grows to about 12 m and has prominently-veined, 15 cm long leaves and small white flowers in late spring. The spice, allspice, frequently used in cooking, is derived from the dried, unripened fruit of the tree.

GROWING A well-drained peaty soil and sunny position are the main requirements. Propagate by layers in spring or by striking softwood in summer. It prefers a wet subtropical climate to tropical coast.

Above ◆ **ALLSPICE**

Below ◆ **ALOE MITRIFORMIS - ONE OF THE MANY SPECIES OF ALOE**

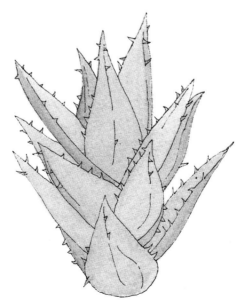

Aloe

ALOE VARIEGATA, PARTRIDGE-BREASTED ALOE

There are hundreds of varieties of these adaptable succulents, many of them suitable for growing indoors. Most have fleshy, spiny-edged, elongated triangular leaves, some forming tightly packed rosettes, others carried on long stems. The tubular flowers are borne on open spikes which appear between the leaves from late winter to summer. One of the most popular and easily grown is the partridge-breasted aloe, *Aloe variegata*, which forms a small rosette of dark grey-green spineless leaves unevenly marked in white transverse bands. The flowers are flesh pink on stems 30 cm in height.

Aloes are used widely for medicinal purposes.

GROWING Best grown in a glasshouse, frame or windowsill in good light. Bright light for all varieties and direct sunlight for those with spiny leaves. Aloes grow well at normal room temperature. To encourage flowering they should be given a short winter rest at a temperature of 10°C or below. Keep soil thoroughly moist when plants are growing but greatly restrict water when they are dormant, while not allowing the soil to dry out completely. Fertilise only during growing period. *Aloe* species prefer a dry atmosphere. Water should not be allowed to stand in the rosettes. Repot annually in spring into a pot one size larger Propagate from offsets and see.ds

Ambrosia

CHENOPODIUM BOTRYS, JERUSALEM OAK

Ambrosia is an annual herb growing to 45 cm with reddish 10 cm leaves looking something like those of the English oak in shape. Flowers are green-hued and the plant is sticky and fragrant.

Ambrosia was used medicinally in Europe but is now grown mainly as a decorative, aromatic herb.

GROWING Plants like full sun, and will grow in any average well-drained soil. They are frost tolerant.

Ambrosia is easily raised from seed and self-sows readily.

American Wormseed

CHENOPODIUM AMBROSIOIDES

This is a slightly larger herb than Ambrosia, growing 50 cm to 1 m high. It is an annual with 13 cm, spear-shaped coarsely toothed leaves. American wormseed has a strong, not altogether pleasant odour. Flowers are very numerous, small, and yellowish-green.

Used medicinally in USA as a vermifuge.

GROWING Grow the plant in full sun in an average, well-drained soil. It is frost tolerant.

Plants are raised easily from seed and self-sow readily.

Angelica

ANGELICA ARCHANGELICA, SYN. A. OFFICINALIS, ARCHANGEL, WILD PARSNIP

This is a stout biennial or perennial herb growing to 2 m or more. Leaves are pinnate and soft green, stems are round, ribbed and hollow. Flowers are yellow-green in umbels, arranged in umbel-like clusters.

Angelica stems can be candied, and

are also used as flavouring when stewing sour fruits such as rhubarb. Tips are cooked in jams and marmalade. The seeds are used in flavouring gin and some liqueurs.

Angelica can be used for potpourri and herb pillows.

GROWING This herb is best suited to cool climate areas where it can be planted in sun or semi-shade. In warm climate areas, semi-shade is essential. Shelter from strong wind is desirable because stems are brittle.

Prepare moist, rich, well-drained soil. Poor soil will result in stunted plants and yellow leaves. The pH range is 6.5 to 8.0. Angelica is frost tolerant, but does not stand high temperatures.

Sow only fresh seed of angelica as older seed will probably not germinate. Transplant when 8 cm high, spacing plants 90 cm apart each way. If allowed to ripen on the plant, seeds will self-sow. As seed is sown in autumn some die-back may occur in cold, wet winters, but new growth will appear in spring. As the plants are usually biennial, new ones should be raised each year, but angelica can be kept as a perennial for some years if flower stems are not allowed to develop.

Propagate also by self-sown seed, or cuttings of the roots. Root cuttings 8 to 10 cm long can be potted up at an angle in 12 cm pots in an equal mixture of sand and peatmoss.

ANGELICA IS OFTEN USED FOR POTPOURRI

Anise

PIMPINELLA ANISUM, COMMON ANISE, SWEET CUMIN

Anise is a dainty annual, native to the Mediterranean and growing 50 to 60 cm high. Leaves vary from the finest linear leaves, to round-toothed leaves, and then, later, to the normal ternately compound, divided leaves. The small, white flowers are in umbels. Like angelica, anise is a member of the parsley family. The fruits are light grey-green and ovoid, and the seeds brown. The stems tend to be weak.

Anise is used to flavour drinks such as Pernod, anisette, ouzo and liqueurs.

STAR ANISE (ILLICIUM VERUM) IS A SMALL EVERGREEN TREE NATIVE TO CHINA, WITH A FLAVOUR SIMILAR TO ANISE

It is still used in cough mixtures. Finely chopped fresh leaves can be added to cooked vegetables, such as carrots, and soups and salads. The seeds or flavouring are used in cakes, sweets and biscuits.

GROWING Anise needs to be planted in a sunny position, preferably sheltered from strong wind. Choose light, fertile, well-drained soil, with a pH around neutral point, 7 to 7.5. Acid soils will need two or three handfuls of ground limestone or dolomite per square metre. This is worked into the soil during digging in late winter.

Anise tolerates frost but needs a dry, warm summer. Water regularly in hot weather. It is not suitable for growing in the hot, wet tropics. In cold areas, a side dressing of fertiliser will help to force on growth so that seeds will ripen in time for harvesting in autumn.

Start seed in spring as soon as the soil is warm. Seeds can be sown in individual pots and planted out when 8 to10 cm high, but as the plants make a fairly long taproot, they do not transplant easily and are usually sown where they are to grow. Thin seedlings to 30 cm apart. Seeds can be sown in clumps for support as the stems are weak. Sow a few seeds in a group about 30 cm in diameter and allow three or four plants to grow on together.

Arrowroot

MARANTA ARUNDINACEA, OBEDIENCE PLANT

Arrowroot is a bushy plant with rhizomatous roots, growing 180 to 200 cm high. The rhizomes are thick and starchy and arrowroot is extracted from them. Stems are slender. Leaves are 10 cm wide to 30 cm long. Flowers are white in branched clusters.

Arrowroot tubers can be eaten, but they are usually treated to make the well-known arrowroot flour.

GROWING Full sun is satisfactory, but on light, exposed, free-draining soils, semi-shade is better. Deep, friable soils are essential; wet, clay soils are not suitable. Heavy dressings of manure or compost, supplemented by a complete fertiliser, are advisable. The plants are gross feeders and rich soil is needed; pH 5.5 to 6.5 should be satisfactory. Plants need a hot, moist, frost-free climate.

Remove flowers as they appear. Harvest rhizomes 10 to 11 months after planting. They are ready when leaves start to die off.

Rhizomes or suckers are planted 15 cm deep, 45 cm apart, in rows 75 cm apart in spring or at the beginning of the rains in the tropics.

Balm

MELISSA OFFICINALIS, SWEET BALM, LEMON BALM

Balm is an upright perennial growing 50 to 60 cm high. The roots spread and can be invasive if not controlled. Stems, like many mints, are square in cross-section. Leaves are green, toothed and look somewhat like the leaves of spearmint, being oval to almost heart-shaped. They have a strong lemon scent. The small white flowers are about 1 cm long.

Balm leaves are used in puddings and sauces, for punches and drinks, and for lemon balm tea. It can also be used to flavour meat. Leaves are valuable for fragrance in potpourris.

GROWING Balm thrives in full sun or part shade, but avoid sites that are overwet and heavily shaded. Soil should be rich and moist with pH 6.0 to 8.0 range. Some lime (ground limestone or dolomite) should be applied at first digging. Ample organic matter should be added.

Frost may burn the leaves of balm and in cold areas the plant will die back in winter but shoot again in spring. Water well in dry periods.

Leaves can be stripped for use fresh at any time. An occasional pruning keeps the bush shapely. Keep any flower buds picked off as they appear. To dry, cut the whole plant back to ground level just as flowers are starting to show. String up branches to dry in an airy place, and rub leaves from the stalks when dry.

Propagate by seed, root divisions or cuttings of firm, new tips 10 cm long. As seed is slow in germinating it is best sown in autumn, say, March or April. Sow in boxes or direct into the growing position. Balm is easily grown from root divisions taken in September and planted in the growing position, allowing 60 to 75 cm between each plant.

For cuttings, cut below a node (leaf joint) and nip off all leaves but the top pair. Strike in a pot of three parts river sand mixed with one part of peatmoss. Plant each cutting about 6 cm deep and firm in the mixture. Keep damp.

LEMON BALM MAKES A DELICIOUS HERBAL TEA AND THE PLANT WILL NATURALISE IN THE GARDEN

Basil

OCIMUM BASILICUM, SWEET OR
COMMON BASIL; *O .B MINUMI,*
BUSH BASIL,
O.B. CITRIODORUM, LEMON
BASIL; *O.B. PURPURASCENS,*
PURPLE BASIL

These are the four annual basils in
general use and for which seed is
usually available, but there are other
varieties of basil, and also lettuce-leaf
basil, which should be correctly named
Perilla frutescens 'Crispa'.

Sweet basil grows from 50 to 75 cm
high, has glossy green leaves, ovate in
shape and 5 to 10 cm long. The whole
plant has a pleasant, spicy clove smell.

Bush basil grows from 15 to 30 cm
and, being a small compact plant with
smaller, shiny leaves, is the best kind
for pot culture. However, the aroma is
not as strong as that of sweet basil.

Lemon basil and purple basil are
similar to sweet basil except that lemon
basil has strongly lemon-scented leaves
and white flowers and purple basil has
purple leaves and attractive mauve and
white flowers.

Basil has a rich, spicy flavour
something like that of cloves. As this
becomes stronger with cooking, use
sparingly. It combines well with garlic,
and is especially delicious with tomato.
Leaves can be stored for a few days in
plastic bags in a refrigerator or
blanched in boiling water and deep
frozen. Flowers and leaves can be used
in salads. The dried leaves have a
flavour more like curry.

GROWING Basil likes warmth, so plant
in a sunny position, or in a warm, semi-
shaded position in hot and tropical areas.
Acid soils will need a dressing of ground
limestone or dolomite. On light soils use 400
to 800 g per m^2, on clay loams from 400 to
1500 g or more. Improve clayey soils by
working in sand. All soils should have ample
organic matter and adequate drainage. A
pH around neutral point, pH 6.0 to 8.0, will
give best results.

Basils dislike cold. Early plantings are not
recommended in frost areas unless the
plants can be protected by cloches or some
other form of protection. Autumn sowings
are only advised in coastal tropical and
similar climates. Last leaves must be
gathered in autumn before cold weather
causes the leaves to yellow.

Basils are raised from seed each year.
The bluish sort of gel on freshly germinating
seeds is normal and not a mould or fungus.
Unless hot frames or glass is available, sow
when danger of frost is over and the ground
has warmed up. Seed is sown thinly 1 cm
deep in drills 3 cm apart. Thin out to 3 cm
apart when seeds germinate and transplant
into permanent positions 30 to 45 cm apart
each way. Thinnings can be pricked out.

For pot culture use a pot 18 to 20 cm in
diameter, with a 3 cm drainage layer, and a
rich potting soil based on sandy loam. Sow
three or four seeds near the centre of the pot
and retain the strongest. The others can be
pricked out 30 cm apart into the open garden
or other pots. Keep well watered, and add
liquid manure from time to time. Avoid using
mixed fertilisers low in nitrogen because they
tend to favour flower rather than leaf
production. Pots kept indoors should be
placed in full sun. Early pinching out of the
tip bud encourages more compact growth.
Leaves can be taken at any time once the
plants are established, which should be
about six weeks from planting out.

To improve bushiness and keep leaves
coming keep flowering tips pinched out. Soil
should be kept just damp, not wet. A liquid
fertiliser given monthly will keep the plants
moving. Choose one with a high nitrogen
ratio. This feeding is particularly necessary
for pot plants grown indoors, but any over-
feeding should be avoided.

PESTO

1 large bunch fresh basil leaves
1 large bunch fresh parsley leaves
4 cloves garlic
3 tablespoons pine nuts
1 teaspoon salt
freshly ground black pepper
⅓ cup (40 g) grated Parmesan cheese
¾ to 1 cup (180 to 250 ml) olive oil

Blend basil, parsley and garlic in a blender
or food processor until finely chopped.
Add pine nuts, salt, pepper and Parmesan.
Blend until a smooth paste is formed.
With motor still running, add oil in a
slow, steady stream until the mixture
becomes a smooth sauce. Do not cook
the sauce for it will separate. Use spooned
over hot pasta, gnocchi, jacket-baked
potatoes or stirred into a minestrone-style
soup.

Makes about 2 cups (500 ml)

Opposite Page: Top ◆ **BASIL AND PASTA
SALAD**
Below Left ◆ **INGREDIENTS FOR MAKING
PESTO**

BASIL AND PASTA SALAD

185 g corkscrew pasta (spirelli)
salt
¼ green cabbage, finely shredded
6 radishes, thinly sliced
1 small green capsicum, thinly sliced
1 punnet (250 g) cherry tomatoes, halved if large
½ telegraph cucumber, thinly sliced
1 ripe avocado, sliced
½ bunch chives and extra basil leaves to garnish

Dressing
2 bunches fresh basil
4 cloves garlic
2 teaspoons Dijon-style mustard
juice ½ lemon
¾ cup (180 ml) olive oil
salt and freshly ground black pepper

Cook pasta in boiling salted water until 'al dente'. Drain and cool. Prepare the vegetables.

To make dressing: Wash basil and strip leaves from stalks (reserve a few for garnish). Place leaves in the container of a food processor with garlic, mustard and half the lemon juice. Blend until finely chopped. Slowly add oil to the container with the motor still running and process until dressing thickens. Season well and add remaining lemon juice to taste. Toss all salad ingredients together in a bowl with dressing. Snip over chives and garnish with reserved basil leaves.

Serves 6

SWEET BASIL (*OCIMUM BASILICUM*)

Bay

LAURUS NOBILIS, SWEET BAY, ROMAN LAUREL

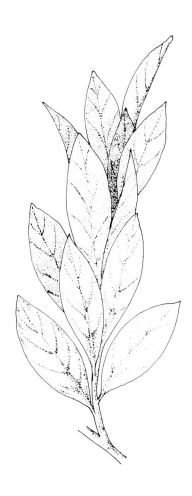

Bay trees make excellent formal or informal tub plants and for this purpose a tree is usually trained as a standard with a single stem, by simply removing the side shoots and suckers.

Leaves are used to flavour food. Usually one leaf is sufficient, either dried or picked fresh, for soups, stews, casseroles, spaghetti dishes, meatloafs, brawns and poultry stuffings. Even rice puddings and custards can be flavoured with bay as a change from vanilla. Bay leaf is used with sprigs of thyme, marjoram and parsley to make a bouquet garni.

GROWING A sunny, open position is most suitable, but bay will tolerate light shade, especially in hot, dry areas. Grow the plant in a reasonably rich, well-manured soil, adequately drained, with a pH range around pH 5.0 to 7.5. Unless soil is strongly acid, liming is unnecessary.

Bay is not hardy to heavy frosts, and if grown in a tub must be moved to a sheltered position in cold weather. It tolerates climates as warm as Brisbane, and winter rain climates such as the Riverina. Provide protection in winter in the colder parts of South Island, New Zealand, otherwise, bay is easy to grow, and can be clipped like a hedge plant to keep it to any desired height or formal shape. Give the plant a dressing of animal manure in late winter and early summer as a mulch.

White wax and pink wax scales can be troublesome. Leaves can be taken at any time. For drying clip from the stalk and spread out on a tray to dry, or hang up a whole branch in an airy shed. Store in air-tight bottles.

Bay can be raised from seed, sown in spring after frost-danger has passed and soil is warm, but plants are usually raised from stem cuttings, suckers or root cuttings. Half-ripe cuttings 10 cm long or hardwood pieces 20 cm long, are suitable. Pot cuttings firmly in damp coarse sand and water regularly. They strike easily, but are slow and may take six months or more before roots develop. They are usually ready to plant out once new leaves have formed on top.

Suckers are side pieces detached complete with roots from round the base of the plant. They can be taken at any time in mild areas. Plant in good potting soil. Root cuttings are pieces of roots taken from near the base of the plant. They should be about 10 cm long. Plant in a slanting position in damp mixture of two parts peatmoss to one part sand.

Bay is an evergreen tree growing 12 to 18 m high. It is not a herb, but the leaves are very popular for flavouring food and so the plant is often listed with herbs. Bay is dioecious, that is, male and female flowers appear on separate plants, and so if seeds are wanted, a male and female tree should be planted. For culinary purposes one plant is enough.

Although growing to a medium-sized tree if unchecked, bay is a tractable plant which can be clipped and kept to any height wanted, from about 2 m upwards. The leaves are leathery, shiny dark green, a narrow, oval shape and about 10 cm long. Leaf stalks and young stems are tinged red. Flowers are small and yellow and the berries black or purple.

SWEET BAY - A BEAUTIFUL EVERGREEN TREE

Bedstraw

GALIUM VERUM, LADY'S BEDSTRAW, YELLOW BEDSTRAW

Bedstraw is a perennial about 1 m high with narrow 3 cm leaves in starry whorls of six to eight leaves. Stems are partly prostrate and so the plant is useful as a ground cover, but must be kept clipped to about 7 to 8 cm high as the season advances. Fragrant, yellow flowers appear in summer.

Bedstraw is a plant that grows easily with almost no attention. It was used when dried to stuff mattresses because it smells like fragrant hay. The juice curdles milk for cheesemaking. The crushed yellow flowers yield a food colour for butter and cheese. It has been used to make cooling summer drinks and for medicine.

GROWING Open or shady ground suits bedstraw, and any reasonable soil; lime is not necessary. Plants are frost tolerant. Bedstraw is usually propagated by division of the clumps.

Bergamot

MONARDA DIDYMA, BEE BALM, OSWEGO TEA, INDIAN PLUME

Bergamot is a handsome perennial growing 60 to 120 cm high in large clumps surmounted by showy 7 cm red flowers. Many cultivars in salmon, pink, magenta, purple, violet, rose-red, crimson, white and scarlet have been developed. There is a dwarf pink flowered sort that grows to only 25 cm.

Bergamot has square stems and toothed leaves to 10 cm long. The flowers are in bracted, rounded heads, each flower long and tubular, rich in nectar, and honeysuckle-like in shape. As it belongs to the mint family, it has spreading runners and will quickly form a large clump.

The whole plant is somewhat pungent and with a citrus aroma. Its common name came from its likeness in smell to *Citrus aurantium* subsp. *bergamia,* the source of the fragrant oil of bergamot. (Oil of bergamot is solely a perfuming agent and in no sense a health herb.) However, the leaves and flowers of the herb bergamot, *Monarda didyma,* are edible. Shredded they make a colourful addition to salads, and are recommended for use with pork, veal and sausages. Use sparingly in casseroles and stews. They are also added to summer drinks and jellies. Bergamot is famous as a tea either on its own or added to normal tea. It has a relaxing, soporific effect.

GROWING Bergamot is a striking background plant in the herb garden and will grow in full sun or semi-shade. If tall, staking may be needed in windy positions. A rich, moist soil is needed, pH range from pH 6.0 to 7.0. Strongly acid soils need liming with ground limestone or dolomite at one to two large double handfuls per square metre. Plenty of organic matter should be added to the soil and an organic mulch used, especially in hot weather.

Animal manure, decaying leaves, straw, grass clippings or compost are suitable. Bergamot is hardy, tolerating temperatures to -29°C.

To harvest bergamot, pick on a hot, dry day and hang head down in an airy place out of direct sun. Plants keep their fragrance for a long time.

Seed is very fine and should be sown in spring on the surface of a seed-tray of finely sifted sandy soil. Press into the surface of the dampened soil and cover with a square of sacking or sheet of heavy brown paper. Water from below by immersing the tray in a shallow dish of water. Prick out when about 8 cm high into 8 to 10 cm pots and later plant out 30 cm apart.

Plants can be divided at any time, although spring is preferable. Replant the vigorous young pieces. Cuttings strike very easily, and most runners will already have roots on them. Plant horizontally in sandy soil, 2 to 3 cm deep. Protect young plants from snails.

BERGAMOT OR OSWEGO TEA. THE TEA WAS DRUNK BY AMERICAN COLONISTS AFTER THE BOSTON TEA PARTY

Borage

BORAGO OFFICINALIS, TALEWART, COOL TANKARD

Borage is a coarse, thick annual, with a single tap-root, and branching hairy stems. Height varies from 30 to 90 cm. In rich soil and well-watered it may develop quickly with large leaves which are susceptible to rust. Leaves are greyish-green, about 10 to 15 cm long, and the whole plant is covered with bristly hairs. Star-like summer flowers in white or blue are most attractive in downward tipped stems, the colours set off by striking black anthers in the centre. Flowering can continue through winter in mild areas.

Borage is still used to add a mild, pleasing cucumber flavour to summer drinks, punches, and wine cups. A single leaf or sprig of leaves can be added or flowers, cut just as they are opening, can be floated on top. Flowers can also be crystallised. Leaves can be added to salads and pickles, or cooked and eaten like spinach. Borage attracts bees, but is not now used medicinally although borage teas were said to be cheering, and useful as diuretics.

GROWING Reasonable care is all that is needed to grow borage, and don't overcoddle is the best advice. If the plants grow more than 60 cm, light stakes might be needed to support them. This is an easy plant for first-time herb gardeners. Plant it in full sun, although it will succeed in places with some light shade. Avoid shady positions. Any reasonable soil will do, but some lime or dolomite is useful on acid soils. A range of about pH 6.0 to 7.5 would be suitable. Organic matter can be added and watering is necessary in dry weather. Gravelly and sandy soils have proved satisfactory.

Borage usually grows from spring to autumn and will tolerate mild frost. In coastal areas, it will sometimes overwinter.

It is easy to propagate borage by seed, in fact borage usually self sows. However overwintering plants can be divided in spring and young tip cuttings sheltered in a frame are fairly easy to strike. Seed should be sown direct in the garden two or three together a few centimetres apart in clumps 45 to 60 cm apart. Leave the strongest seedling only at each position. If transplanting, do so early before the tap-root develops too far.

PURPLE-FLOWERED BORAGE (BORAGO OFFICINALIS)

Burnet

POTERIUM SANGUISORBA, SALAD BURNET

Burnet is a dainty, graceful perennial with basal rosettes of feathery, soft green leaves. The rosettes usually grow 15 to 30 cm high and flowers can grow 15 to 45 cm higher. Leaf colour varies from yellow-green to blue-green on the outside of the rosettes. Red to purple flowers growing on small, thimble-like heads appear in the second summer.

The flavour is similar to nuts or cucumber, and burnet is used in much the same way as borage. Leaves are added to salads, soups, iced drinks, vinegar and can also be chopped finely and blended with butter, peanut butter and cream cheese. Use only young leaves as older leaves tend to be bitter.

Burnet makes an attractive medium size edging plant for a border.

GROWING Full sun is needed to grow burnet, but any average well-drained soil will do. Keep plant well watered in dry, warm weather but water less in winter or crown rot could develop. Lime or dolomite is

SALAD BURNET (*POTERIUM SANGUISORBA*)

Caper

CAPPARIS SPINOSA

Strictly, caper is not a herb, but it is a condiment and capers and caper sauce are well known. This is a straggly, spiny shrub growing from 90 to 150 cm. Leaves are roundish to oval-shaped, 5 cm long, flowers are white from 6 to 8 cm across with long purple stamens. Plant is usually deciduous in temperate areas, but elsewhere evergreen. The flower buds have a distinctive pungent flavour and are pickled and marketed as capers.

GROWING This is a glasshouse plant in cold areas, and needs in any garden a full sun position. Soil should be perfectly drained and is, ideally, sandy loam with some organic matter. Caper does well in dry, rocky areas with Mediterranean-type climate as in inland Australia, and also in warm coastal areas. A neutral pH should be suitable. Therefore acid coastal soils would need a fairly heavy dressing of lime or dolomite, say from $\frac{1}{2}$ to 1 kg per square metre.

Caper will stand only the lightest frost and thrives in warm frost-free areas. Water when required in dry areas. Harvest flower buds before they reach full size and start to burst.

In warm climates caper is raised easily from seed. Sow in drills in late winter or in February in tropics, 5 cm apart, thin to 5 cm in the drill and plant out when 8 to 10 cm high spacing 1 m apart each way. In cooler areas take ripe shoots and propagate by striking in river sand under glass, preferably with the pot itself covered with polythene film over wire hoops.

necessary in all except alkaline soils. A pH around neutral point (pH 7.0) is desirable.

Burnet is hardy and will tolerate temperatures as low as -35°C. It makes good growth in winter. A heavy mulch, kept away from the crown of the plant, will help to keep the soil moist in dry periods. Keep untidy flower stems pinched out at tips.

Burnet is usually grown from seed which germinates easily. It is best to sow in autumn or spring and when plants are 5 to 6 cm high, thin to 23 to 30 cm apart. Thinnings can be transplanted. Tip cuttings should strike readily, and older plants can be divided by cutting away some of the basal rosettes.

Caraway

CARUM CARVI

Caraway is a biennial plant which may grow as an annual or, in mild climates, as a perennial. If sown in autumn, in March, it will usually grow 45 to 60 cm high and will flower in the summer, from November to January. Spring plantings, on the other hand, tend to show the biennial characteristics, growing to 20 cm in the first summer. Plants then die back over winter, shoot again the following spring, and flower and fruit by midsummer. Leaves are divided with lacy leaflets and flowers are white, occasionally pink, in umbels.

Once used freely medicinally, caraway is now used mainly to flavour biscuits, cakes, breads, cheese and cottage cheese, liqueurs and vegetables such as beetroot and cabbage. The roots are sometimes cooked like carrots.

GROWING Full sun and a sheltered, well-drained position is recommended. Any average soil will suit, even clay loams, provided the drainage is good, particularly in winter. The soil should not be too acid,

pH about 5.5 to 6.5. Strongly acid soils need lime or dolomite dressings, and a handful per square metre would be advantageous on light, sandy loams. Add also some organic matter and use a mulch of animal manure in summer to retain moisture. Caraway is hardy and will tolerate winter temperatures to as low as -35°C.

Normal garden care only is needed. Keep weeds chipped away. Water regularly in hot weather and retain an organic mulch.

Propagate caraway from seed sown where the plants are to grow in spring or autumn. Autumn sowings give earlier results. As the seedlings do not transplant easily, sowing in boxes or trays is not advisable. Sow seed thinly 1 cm deep in drills 30 cm apart and when 8 cm high, thin-out to 20-23 cm apart. Keep the bed damp as seed may be slow to germinate — up to 30 days or more. (For a quicker growing method, see 'Parsley').

Top ◆ **CARAWAY, A HERB WITH AN UNMISTAKEABLE FLAVOUR**
Above ◆ **LEAVES AND SEEDS OF THE CARAWAY PLANT (CARUM CARVI)**

Cardamom

ELETTARIA CARDAMOMUM

Cardamom is a tall, herbaceous perennial and a member of the ginger family. It grows from 2 to 3 m or more in height and has a stout, fleshy rhizome and green leaves 9 cm wide to 75 cm long which are silky beneath. The flowering stems are shorter, up to 60 cm long, and spread horizontally near the ground. The small flowers are white, striped pink. The egg-shaped fruits are 1 to 2 cm long with dark red-brown seeds. Other related plants are often confused with true cardamom and sometimes sold as substitutes.

Cardamom seeds are used to flavour cakes, pastries, breads, curries and even coffee. Sausages, jellies, custards, fruit salads, some liqueurs and spiced wine are also flavoured with cardamom.

GROWING A warm, completely frost-free aspect, and partial overhead shade is ideal. Protect from strong winds. Cardamom needs tropical or warm subtropical temperatures. A rich, moist soil with a pH of about 6.5 is best. Strongly acid soils will need dressings of ground limestone or dolomite at 500 to 750 g per square metre. Add plenty of organic matter such as compost or animal manure and work into the soil before planting.

Keep plants free of weeds and mulch with a heavy layer of organic matter — straw, sawdust, spent mushroom compost or manure. Water copiously all through the growing season, but withhold water and keep on the dry side in winter. Harvest by picking the fruit *before* it is fully ripe. Wash fruit and spread out in hessian trays in the sun to dry and bleach.

Propagate from seed, which may take 2 to 3 months to germinate or by division of the strong, long rhizomes. Seed is sown in nursery beds or trays. The soil can be 4 parts loam, 1 part organic matter — manure, compost or peatmoss — and 1 part sand. Sow seed thinly and transplant when 8 to 10 cm high either into the growing bed or into 15 cm pots, for subsequent transplanting. When planting out seedlings or divisions of the rhizomes, place 3 or 4 plants in clumps, each piece being 15 cm apart and space the clumps about 3 m apart each way.

THE OVAL PODS OF CARDAMOM

Catnip

NEPETA CATARIA, CATNEP, CATMINT

Catnip is a straggly herb growing from 60 to 90 cm high. Leaves are more or less heart-shaped green above and silvery-grey beneath because of the down on their surface. Stems are square. Flowers are two-lipped white to pale pink with purple dots. They are carried on straggly stems in many flowered whorls.

Catnip leaves can be made into a tea. The dried leaves and flowers are often used to stuff cloth mice for cats to play with. The herb has a long history of use in medicine and is still prescribed today.

GROWING Catnip suits a sunny or semi-shady position. It will grow in quite poor soil, but does much better in a sandy loam enriched with organic matter. Some lime or dolomite should be worked into acid soils for a pH range of 6.0 to 8.0. Provide perfect drainage. Catnip is hardy to -35°C.

CATMINT (NEPETA SPECIES)

Catnip is a member of the mint family, and so needs no more special care than garden mint. Moderately water in dry spells and give some nitrogen feeding in spring, such as a light sprinkling of cool poultry manure. Cut back hard after flowering.

Catnip is easily propagated by division of the plants in spring or autumn. Stem cuttings usually strike readily. Plants can be raised easily from seed in spring. Cuttings, divisions and young seedlings should be covered with wire netting to protect them from cats, which like to roll on the plants, pull them up or eat the leaves.

Chamomile

MATRICARIA RECUTITA, SYN. M. CHAMOMILLA, GERMAN, TRUE OR WILD CHAMOMILE; CHAMAEMELUM NOBILE, SYN. ANTHEMIS NOBILIS, ROMAN, ENGLISH, PERENNIAL OR GARDEN CHAMOMILE

There are other common names for German chamomile, such as single chamomile or pinheads. It is an aromatic annual herb which grows 15 to 60 cm high. The stems branch freely and are upright or prostrate, with feathery leaves with linear leaflets. The flowers are typical, white daisy flowers with about fifteen white petals (ray-florets) often reflexed from the small cluster of green-yellow true flowers in the centre.

German chamomile, *Matricaria,* is the one usually used medicinally. Chamomile tea, thought to be a curative and soothing drink is made from the dried flowers. They are also used in vermouths and apéritifs.

Roman chamomile, *Chamaemelum,* is a low growing, spreading perennial, starting as a flat rosette of radiating stems to about 8 cm high. With later growth and flowering, plants may reach 30 cm. Stems are hairy, branch freely and have many lacy leaves divided into linear segments. Daisy-like flowers with yellow centres and eighteen white petals appear in

GERMAN CHAMOMILE (*MATRICARIA CHAMOMILLA*)

summer. The leaves and stems are covered with grey-green down and when walked on emit a strong, pleasant fragrance.

The flowers of Roman chamomile can be used to prepare medicinal infusions. The plants make a fragrant ground cover. If grown as a lawn, plants can be cut back with a mower provided the blades are set high, above 6 cm.

GROWING German chamomile, *Matricaria,* can be grown in sun or semi-shade. It is not fussy about soil types but should never be allowed to dry right out. It needs well-drained soil.

Some animal manure and a low nitrogen fertiliser (No. 5 or Q 5) will help the plants along. Flowers should be cut before the petals bend right down. Dry in a warm, dry place, or oven, and store in plastic bags.

Roman or perennial chamomile, *Chamaemelum,* does best in full sun but will grow in part shade. The double flowered form (best for medicinal uses) does best in a rich, moist, fairly heavy clay loam, but the wild single form seems to flourish better in sandy loams. Both types need well-drained soil. Very acid soils might need a dressing of lime or dolomite worked in at the first digging in late winter, pH 6.0 to 7.5 being suitable. Plants are hardy and tolerate frosts to -29°C.

If planting a chamomile lawn, dig the ground during winter. Rake lime or dolomite, if required, into the top 5 or 6 cm and level the soil surface. Keep the area watered and

cultivate as weeks or grasses appear. When weed eradication has been successful, broadcast the seed over the area, rake in and keep damp in the early stages. Thereafter keep free of weed and clip off flower heads if they appear.

Propagate German chamomile by seed sown in spring. Press seeds into the top of a fine seedling mixture in a box or tray. When four leaves have developed prick out into 8 cm pots or beds, spacing them 8 cm apart, or plant in flowering positions. As the stems develop, cuttings can be taken and will strike quite easily if firmly planted in a pot of half sand/ half peatmoss. Roman chamomile germinates readily from seed sown in spring, and chamomile lawns are often started with seed. For double flowers, division of the older plants is more reliable because seed produces a large proportion of single flowering plants.

Divisions can be taken in early spring. Cuttings planted in pots of coarse sand will strike quickly.

Chervil

ANTHRISCUS CEREFOLIUM

Chervil is a hardy annual with finely divided leaves rather like parsley, but less robust, and paler in colour. Height varies from 30 to 45 cm or more. Flowers are in flat white umbels. The varieties with curly leaves are favoured. If sowing seed, keep seed only from plants with the curliest leaves. Because it has a large tap root, chervil sometimes carries over into the second year, but it is not strictly biennial.

Chervil, with chives, is one of the herbs used in the French mixture *fines herbes.* The flavour is sometimes described as being like parsley, but sweeter, or more piquant, with a suggestion of anise. Chervil should be used fresh either as a garnish in small sprigs or chopped fine for addition to salads and soups. It has been called the gourmet's parsley and is used fresh in many ways. In the past the roots were eaten, the leaves were cooked like spinach and it was used medicinally.

CHERVIL (*ANTHRISCUS CEREFOLIUM*)

Chicory

CICHORIUM INTYBUS, SUCCORY, BARBE DE CAPUCHIN

Chicory is a tall, stout, somewhat ungainly perennial that starts as an upright rosette of leaves that are variable but usually rather like dandelion. The limbs tend to branch widely and have few leaves so that they look bare and straggly. The flowers are rich sky-blue. Pink and white varieties exist. Plant has a thick, white, long root, looking much like parsnip. The overall height in flower may vary from 100 to 180 cm.

Chicory is used raw or cooked as a vegetable. The roots can be cooked and eaten like parsnip, and are used as a flavour for coffee or as a coffee substitute.

GROWING A sunny situation suits chicory best. Because of their height, plants can go at the back of a herb border or in the centre of island beds. A reasonably well-drained soil enriched with organic matter is best. The New Zealand writer Gillian Painter states that chicory likes 'a light, chalky soil' — i.e. a limed soil, and the American la

CHICORY - LOOKS RATHER LIKE DANDELION

GROWING Partial shade is essential for chervil because it favours cooler, damp conditions. It is not suitable for hot, dry or tropical climates. Chervil can grow in poorer soils but does best in a humus-enriched, well-drained loamy soil, probably with pH 5.0 to 6.0. Liming would be needed only on strongly acid soils.

In England, chervil is sown in February, so germination could be counted on at almost any time of the year in Australia and New Zealand. In warmer districts, sow in late summer and autumn for growth during the cooler months. In strong sun chervil leaves go pink and shrivel. Side dressings of poultry manure or nitrogen fertiliser will promote heavy growth. Keep flower heads cut off, but allow them to develop if seed is wanted. Harvest leaves from the outside of the clump. Discard any discoloured ones. Leaves can be taken at any time from about six to eight weeks after sowing.

Propagate chervil by seed sown on the surface of permanent beds and firmed in. The beds should be well-drained, fined down before sowing and kept damp at all times, preferably with morning sprays, after sowing. Thin to 30 cm between plants and rows. Seed, if fresh, should germinate in seven to ten or twelve days. Successive sowings at monthly intervals provide a continuous supply. Seed must be fresh. Small plants may transplant, but direct sowing is more reliable.

Motte test showed that chicory does best in soils with a pH range of pH 6.0 to 8.0.

Chicory is hardy. Most Australian and New Zealand climates are suitable. It should tolerate the tropics, but try sowing at the beginning of the dry season, about March, and regularly watering during growth. As chicory has long, large roots, the soil should be deeply dug and enriched with cool animal manure. During growth, give side dressings of a complete fertiliser and repeat each spring and new year.

For coffee substitute or additive the roots are dug in autumn, sliced, dried, roasted and ground.

For greens, a small quantity of leaves are finely shredded and added to cooked leafy vegetables or salads, but as the flavour is bitter, it is more usual to blanch the leaves. The variety witloof is grown for blanching. The plants are sown and spaced as below, and are dug in autumn, about early April. The leaves are cut back to just above the crown. The roots are trimmed by cutting off the lower end to leave them 20 to 22 cm long and they are then left out in a shady spot for two weeks.

Then stand them upright in a deep box and cover the crowns to 20 cm deep with sandy soil and store the boxes in a cellar or dark place. A temperature of about 16°C is best. If all light is excluded the leaves will be creamy white and can be picked as soon as they show through the soil.

Sow chicory seed 3 cm deep in drills 30 to 45 cm apart in September. Thin to a spacing of 15 to 20 cm between plants. If handled carefully thinnings can be transplanted. Older clumps can be divided and replanted in autumn.

Chives

**ALLIUM SCHOENOPRASUM,
GRASS ONION,
ALLIUM TUBEROSUM, CHINESE
CHIVES, GARLIC CHIVES**

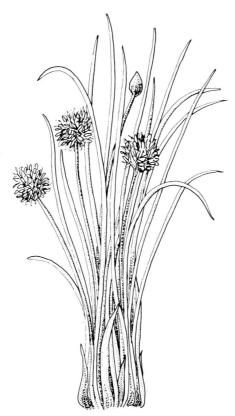

Chives are miniature, delicately flavoured, perennial onions, which if untrimmed will grow to 60 cm. Most are trimmed regularly to about 15 cm high. The small bulbs multiply into quite large clumps. The leaves are hollow, slender, bright green and tubular. The flowers are an attractive rosy-mauve.

Chinese chives are like chives except that the leaves are flat. The flowers are white, starry, arranged in umbels, and fragrant, but the plants are not as vigorous as chives. Leaves have a mild garlic flavour and the bulbs elongate from a stout underground stem or rhizome. Use as for chives where a garlic flavour is wanted.

The fine leaves of both kinds of chives are chopped up and added to salads, used in sandwiches, or in egg dishes such as scrambled eggs or omelettes where a mild onion or garlic flavour is wanted. Chives are so attractive whether in leaf or in flower that they are frequently used as small edging plants in the flower or vegetable garden.

GROWING Chives will grow satisfactorily in sun or partial shade, but full sun is better. Chives are frost hardy, tolerating temperatures as low as -37°C.

For good results, plants need a fairly rich soil, regular moisture and good drainage, pH range from pH 6.0 to 8.0. Apply a preplanting ration of superphosphate (30 g per square metre) in more acid soils.

Dig the soil, add some sand to heavy clay soils, and work in the superphosphate, or bonemeal for those who prefer organic fertilisers. Some cool poultry manure or nitrogen fertiliser is advantageous. Weeds should be suppressed and adequate water given at all times. To harvest, cut the leaves, but not too low down and if possible clip off the older, taller leaves leaving the younger ones intact. Continuous low cutting will starve the bulbs so that they die out.

Chives are raised easily from seed. Sow in drills 20 to 30 cm apart and 3 mm deep, and thin to the same distance between plants when they are 10 cm high. Alternatively, clumps of bulbs can be bought and pulled apart gently to make planting sets of 4 to 8 bulbs to be planted 20 to 30 cm apart. Clumps should be divided every second or third year.

Above ◆ **CHIVES IN FLOWER**
Opposite ◆ **SWEET CICELY CAN BE USED
AS A SUGAR SUBSTITUTE**

Cicely

MYRRHIS ODORATA, SWEET CICELY, MYRRH

Sweet cicely is a decorative perennial growing 60 to 90 cm high with delicately lacy soft green leaves with small toothed leaflets. The leaves turn purple before they die back in autumn. The small whitish, fluffy flowers are in compound umbels. The fruits are 2 cm long, ribbed and shiny black. A true herbaceous perennial, the plant dies back for a couple of months in winter.

Leaves can be chopped and added to salads as can the sliced green seeds. For fish dishes, sweet cicely is chopped up fine and blended with butter and lemon juice. Its greatest value is as a sugar substitute or use with fruit. Leaves added to stewing fruit, or minced for use in fruit salad, reduce acidity and the amount of sugar needed. Seeds are used in Chartreuse, and are probably still considered to have a health value.

GROWING Sweet cicely does best in shade or semi-shade. The leaves turn pink with sunburn in exposed positions. Sweet cicely is hardy and withstands cold to -29°C.

As sweet cicely makes tap roots, the soil should be deeply dug. The pH range is about pH 5.0 to 7.0 so that liming is necessary only on very acid soils. Compost or animal manure should be forked into the soil and a spring and summer mulch will retain moisture. Drainage needs to be adequate, and watering should be regular in dry periods.

Plants can be raised from seed which may take eight or nine months to germinate. This time could be shortened by stratifying the seed as soon as it is ripe. To do this, seeds are mixed with damp peatmoss in a closed plastic bag and stored in a cool spot where winters are cold, or in the warm, dairy shelf of a refrigerator. A temperature of 5°C should be satisfactory. Sow the seed in early spring, about August, spacing them 45 to 50 cm apart.

Plants can also be divided in spring or autumn. Separate the root clumps with a sharp knife and replant 45 to 50 cm apart. Shorten straggling long roots if necessary.

Comfrey

SYMPHYTUM OFFICINALE, KNITBONE, BONESET, BRUISEWORT

Varieties and hybrids of symphytums have caused some confusion. Russian comfrey (S. x *uplandicum* syn. S. *peregrinum*) is a hybrid of *S. asperum* and the common comfrey (S. *officinale*). It is a larger, coarser plant. Caucasian comfrey (S. *caucasicum*) is by some claimed to be superior and juicier.

Common comfrey is a large-leafed perennial with strong root development. It can be a nuisance if not kept under control, as any piece of root will sprout and grow. Average height is 60 to 90 cm. The lower leaves may be from 25 to 60 cm long, with much smaller leaves higher up the plant. Flowers in drooping, curling clusters vary from purple through blue and pink to cream.

Warnings have been given that although comfrey has always been prized for its valuable vitamin content it may be unsafe to eat or take internally. External use as a poultice is still permissible. Comfrey makes a

COMFREY (*SYMPHYTUM OFFICINALE*)

valuable liquid manure and compost addition.

GROWING Best growth is made when comfrey is planted in shade. A rich, damp soil gives best results. Use ample compost and/or animal manure for feeding and keep flower buds picked off to prevent seeding. Comfrey is hardy and should tolerate all but the severest weather in Australia and New Zealand, but do not allow plants to dry out.

Comfrey can be grown from seed sown in spring, but is also divided in spring or autumn, or grown from root cuttings. Almost any piece of root will strike.

Coriander

**CORIANDRUM SATIVUM,
CHINESE PARSLEY, CILANTRO**

Coriander is an annual which grows from 25 to 50 or 60 cm high, the ultimate height depending on the soil, food and water supply. The lower leaves are deeply cut, more or less oval in outline, but as the upper leaves develop they are threadlike or linear. The flowers grow in flattish umbels with fertile flowers and larger petals mainly round the outside. Colour varies from white to pink or mauve-tinged pink. The fruits, often called seeds, are about 3 to 4 mm long, rounded and ribbed on the outside, at first green but later turning pale yellow-brown.

Coriander leaves are used in salads and pickles, or can be candied. The seeds have a sweet spicy taste and are used in curries, cakes, biscuits, gingerbread, pickles, bread, liqueurs and vermouths, fish dishes and other foods.

GROWING Full sun suits coriander best, but shade plants from afternoon sun in hot summer areas. Coriander is not fussy about soil requirements, but does well in any average soil provided it has adequate drainage, pH range from pH 5.0 to 7.0. Lime would be needed only on strongly acid soils. Coriander is hardy and will grow through the winter except in very cold areas. Where frosts occur, sow under glass for early germination.

Seeds can be sown at almost any time in moderate climates or in spring in cold areas. They germinate quickly in 5 to 10 days, two plants arising from each. If leaves are to be used, sow seeds once a fortnight. If transplanting plants separate the seedlings before they develop too long a taproot. The leaves can be used when the plants are as small as 15 cm high. If sown direct, space the rows 25 cm apart and thin to 25 cm between plants.

Flowering takes about two months from sowing and as the seeds begin to ripen (really the fruits) they change from green to grey or even yellow-brown. Do not harvest when wet. Cut off fruiting heads and dry in a sunny dry spot on shallow trays.

Above ◆ **CORIANDER LEAVES AND ROOT (*CORIANDRUM SATIVUM*)**
Below ◆ **CORIANDER FLOWERS**

THAI CHICKEN SALAD

4 to 6 boneless chicken breasts
¼ cup (60 ml) rice wine vinegar
1 tablespoon light soy sauce
1 tablespoon raw sugar
2 tablespoons fresh coriander leaves
1 tablespoon sesame seed oil

Salad Vegetables
1 red and 1 green capsicum, seeded and finely sliced
½ bunch shallots, finely sliced on the diagonal
1 large carrot, julienned
½ telegraph cucumber, peeled and julienned
2 tomatoes, peeled, seeded and cut into eighths
1 small head cos lettuce

Dressing
3 tablespoons rice wine vinegar
1 tablespoon Japanese horseradish paste or chopped horseradish
1 teaspoon sugar
freshly ground black pepper
3 tablespoons walnut oil

Garnish
3 tablespoons each chopped coriander, mint and basil
½ bunch chives
2 tablespoons sesame seed, toasted

Cut each chicken breast into three long strips. Place in a glass or ceramic bowl and add vinegar, soy sauce, sugar and coriander. Toss to combine, cover and refrigerate overnight.

Heat sesame oil in a wok and stir-fry chicken pieces over high heat until just cooked. Turn out onto a plate and prepare salad vegetables.

To make the dressing, combine first four ingredients in a bowl. Whisk in oil until combined.

Toss vegetables together with half the dressing. Arrange in the centre of each individual plate with a few small cos leaves. Divide chicken strips between the plates, arranging them over the salad. Sprinkle each plate with a little more dressing and garnish each with fresh herbs and toasted sesame seeds.

Serves 4 to 6

Costmary

CHRYSANTHEMUM BALSAMITA, SYNS. *C. MAJUS*, *TANACETUM BALSAMITA*, ALECOST, MINT GERANIUM

Costmary is a coarse silvery-grey perennial with large, oblong, round-tipped, bluntly toothed leaves, 15 to 18 cm or more long and about 5 cm wide. Depending on season and soil, it grows from 60 to 120 cm high or more. Leaves have a pleasant mint smell when crushed. Flowers have only tiny white ray florets and look like round yellow buttons. Roots spread outwards and make clumps.

Leaves are used as a garnish or

Left ◆ **THAI CHICKEN SALAD**
Above ◆ **FRAGRANT SACHETS ARE MADE FROM COSTMARY LEAVES**

brewed as a tea and when dried are used in sausages or with poultry or veal. The leaves are also used in sachets for fragrance in linen cupboards.

GROWING Costmary tolerates sunny and shady positions, but shade-grown plants have less fragrance and no flowers. Almost any soil will do, though free-draining sandy loams are best. Suitable pH range is about pH 5.5 to 7.0. Costmary will tolerate cold down to -29°C. In cooler areas costmary will, like many perennials, die right back in winter, but the roots are not killed by snow or hard frost and will shoot again in spring.

Divide the clumps every second or third year in late winter, early spring and plant firmly 50 to 60 cm apart each way. Use the younger vigorous stools round the clump and discard old ones in the centre. Divisions are planted in spring and autumn, and can be grown as indoor pot plants if given a sunny window ledge. Inside, don't allow stems to develop, cut them down as they appear; a 10 to 12 cm pot is large enough. Do not over-water.

COWSLIP

Above ◆ **WATERCRESS**
Below ◆ **WATERCRESS SOUP, AND WATERCRESS AND SMOKED SALMON LOG**

Cowslip

PRIMULA VERIS, HERB-PETER, PAIGLE, PEGGLE, KEY FLOWER

A small perennial, spring-flowering herb whose crinkled, downy, tongue-shaped leaves tend to lie flat on the ground in a rosette. Clusters of yellow or pale yellow flowers emerge from the top of a stalk about 30 cm high in spring.

Cowslips are still made into wine and used in some medicines. The flowers can be candied, and leaves and flowers can be used in salads. Dried flowers and roots are used in a tea.

GROWING Plants prefer a shady position, and enjoy organic-rich soils, pH 5.0 to 7.0 and higher since plants thrive on calcareous soils overseas, as well as clay. Cowslips are hardy, tolerating heavy frosts.

Cowslips can be grown easily from root divisions in autumn. When sown in sandy loam in pans or boxes as soon as available, seed germinates readily, and seedlings can be transplanted 15 to 20 cm apart.

Cress

LIPIDIUM SATIVUM, GARDEN CRESS, *BARBAREA VERNA* SYN. *B. PRAECOX*, LAND CRESS, AMERICAN CRESS, UPLAND CRESS NASTURTIUM, *OFFICINALE* SYN. *RORIPPA NASTURTIUM-AQUATICUM*, WATER CRESS

Garden cress is a small, quick growing annual with a maximum height of 30 to 60 cm. Basal leaves are feathery and toothed, but stem leaves are linear and entire. This is the salad plant which is cut young and used with mustard. Like all cress, it contains plenty of Vitamin C.

GROWING Garden cress tolerates full sun or semi-shade and is often grown indoors on a sunny windowsill in pans or trays. Soil is not necessary if grown for salad use. The seeds can be sprouted on any soft damp surface such as cotton wool, blotting paper or cloth etc. If grown on for seed the plants should be in a reasonable, well-drained soil suitable for seedling ◆

raising. A dressing of dolomite can be added to acid soils. At no time must the soil dry out. Keep under cover if hard frosts threaten, but seedlings will grow in the winter. Broadcast the seed quite thickly and do not thin out. A fresh sowing every second week will keep up a continuous supply. Mustard is sown four days later. Keep cress moist and harvest when 5 to 7 cm high.

Land cress is a biennial herb. It flowers and seeds in the second year or is grown as an annual. Height is about 60 to 90 cm growing from a rosette of long leaves about 30 cm wide. Leaves are about 15 cm long, feathery, with an oval lobe at the end. The small cross-shaped, bright yellow flowers are followed by a beaked silique, about 5 cm long. It is more pungent than garden cress, less delicate in flavour than water cress.

GROWING Land cress is not fussy and will grow in sun or semi-shade. Soil should be average and if enriched with animal

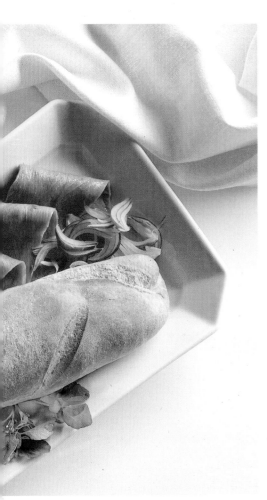

manure will produce abundant succulent leaves of better flavour. If the soil becomes too dry, plants may run up to seed. A little dolomite can be added to acid soils. Land cress will grow through winter and summer, but in cold areas a cloche cover will promote better growth. Sow seed in late summer for winter-spring harvesting and in spring for summer-autumn crops. Land cress needs only average care. Water regularly in dry weather. Should any flowering stems appear, remove them if you want continued leaf production. Should plants go to seed the young seedlings can be eaten or allowed to grow on. In good conditions plants multiply rapidly.

Watercress is a hardy perennial aquatic herb with floating and ascending stems that produce roots readily at each leaf-joint. Juvenile leaves are oval or heart-shaped, mature leaves are pinnate with round or oval leaflets numbering from 3 to 11. Flowers are white and produce 10 to 12 mm siliques with seeds. Can be grown in wet soil but water must not be stagnant.

Like other cresses, watercress is used for salads, garnishes and sandwiches. It is rich in iron and is used in a cress-vinegar tea recommended for headaches, and also in soups.

GROWING Watercress should be grown in the shade, where the leaves will be a rich, appetising green. In the sun they turn brown. A rich loam at the base of a gently running stream is best, but water must be known to be pure. Similar conditions can be simulated in an old bath or trough half-filled with loamy soil, then filled up with water. This should be carefully siphoned or drained off and replaced with fresh, clean water each week. Watercress is most easily propagated from pieces, but not from plants in polluted streams or streams that run through sheep pastures. It is safer to raise new plants from seed, sown and lightly covered in a seed-box or pan. Transplant to permanent water-bed when 5 to 10 cm high. Cut back any flowering stems that appear. If white butterfly caterpillars are troublesome, cover the bed with shade cloth to keep out the butterflies.

Cumin

CUMINUM CYMINUM SYN. C. ODORUM

Cumin is a small annual herb growing only 15 to 30 cm high. The stems are slender, branching, tending to be angular with left-stalks clasping the stems. Deep green leaves are lacy, and branching is threadlike. The flowers are white or rose-pink in compound unbelliferous heads in summer. The 'seeds' are really the fruits and look rather like straightened caraway seeds, but lighter coloured and bristly instead of smooth.

Cumin 'seeds' are ground and used in curry powders, and in many other ways to flavour food, for example, in soups, stews, pickles and chutneys. Cumin has been used in veterinary medicine.

GROWING A rich, well-drained loam is needed, for example, a sandy loam that has been enriched with ample organic matter such as animal manure or compost. Around pH 6.0 should be most suitable and dolomite should be added to acid soils.

Cumin is hardy but should be grown in pots in a hot frame where summer seasons are short. It needs full sun. In very hot, dry areas cumin may not do well and perhaps a semi-shaded position could be tried, as cumin has been grown in areas such as Turkestan.

Force plants along quickly with ample water. Keep free of weeds. If set out early, cloches are an advantage.

Raise from seed in pots and transplant after thinning without disturbing the root-ball, or sow direct into prepared bed in warm areas. As the plants need a minimum of four months to mature, it is necessary to start them with heat under glass.

Dandelion

TARAXACUM OFFICINALE, SYN. LEONTODON TARAXACUM

Dandelion is a perennial herb, but if cultivated it is usually grown as an annual. Height is to 45 cm, but leaves grow as a flattened rosette. Leaves grow to as much as 30 cm long with ragged edges and more or less triangular lobes. Flowers are bright orange yellow, 3 cm across, with a stalk that is a long, hollow tube.

Dandelion leaves are used as a vegetable and in salads. The roots are washed, dried and ground as a caffeine-free substitute for coffee.

GROWING Dandelions grow in an open sunny position. Flowers do not open in shade. For robust plants and succulent leaves, a rich, loamy soil is best. Dress soil with ground limestone or dolomite if strongly acid. Fork in animal manure or compost. A pH 6.0 to 8.0 is best. Dandelions tolerate heavy frost.

Little care is needed for dandelions apart from watering in dry weather. Pick leaves from autumn onwards. Keep flower heads picked off unless seed is wanted. Choose only the best plants for seed. Leaves are improved by blanching. Clumps of old plants can be divided and replanted, but seed germinates readily. Sow in spring in dri lls 45 cm apart and thin out to 30 cm apart, or sow in hills, with 30 to 40 cm between each hill.

Dill

ANETHUM GRAVEOLENS SYN. PEUCEDANUM GRAVEOLENS

DILL LEAVES

Seeds can be steeped in vinegar to make dill vinegar and the plant is added to cucumber to make dill pickles.

GROWING Full sun is needed to grow dill. The soil should be worked into a fine tilth and have moisture-holding organic matter added, particularly where soil is sandy. Good drainage is necessary, but the pH tolerance is wide.

The long single stem of dill needs wind protection. Being a spring-summer grower dill does not have to withstand cold temperatures. Keep the soil damp at all times.

Leaves cut just before flowering are at their peak for flavour.

Dill is raised only from seed which should be sown direct into the bed where plants are to grow. The slender taproot makes transplanting extremely difficult. Dill can also be grown in clumps spaced 30 cm apart.

Dill is an annual growing 60 to 120 cm tall. Its blue-green leaves are finely cut into thread-like branching segments. The flowers are small and yellow and arranged in flat umbels about 15 cm across. The fruits, called seeds, are oval, flat and brown, and mature in about 5 to 6 weeks.

Leaves are picked to flavour salads, potatoes, green vegetables and many dishes.

DANDELIONS

FLATHEAD AND DILL PARCELS WITH DILL SAUCE, AND BABY SQUASH WITH DILL

FLATHEAD AND DILL PARCELS WITH DILL SAUCE

8 small fillets flathead (or other white-fleshed fish)
8 English spinach leaves, blanched and stems removed
grated rind 1 lemon
freshly ground black pepper
¼ telegraph cucumber, julienned
1 carrot, peeled and julienned
1 bunch fresh dill
30 g firm butter
8 sheets filo pastry
155 g unsalted butter, melted

Dill Sauce
3 egg yolks
3 tablespoons lemon juice
salt and pepper
185 g unsalted butter
2 tablespoons chopped fresh dill

Remove skin and any bones from fillet. Place each fillet on a blanched spinach leaf. Sprinkle with lemon rind and black pepper. Arrange strips of cucumber and carrot, and a sprig of dill over each fillet. Cut butter into 8 slivers. Place a sliver on each fillet. Wrap up each fish with its spinach leaf, tucking the thin tail end up inside.

Brush a sheet of pastry with melted butter. Place a fish bundle at the end of the sheet and wrap up like a parcel. Set on a greased baking tray and brush with melted butter. Repeat with remaining fillets and pastry. Bake in a 190°C (375°F) for 12 to 15 minutes or until golden brown. Serve hot with sauce.

To make sauce, place egg yolks in a food processor with 1 tablespoon lemon juice. Season with salt and pepper. Melt butter until foaming. With the motor running, pour in the sizzling butter, slowly at first, until a thick sauce forms. Add remaining lemon juice and stir through dill. Spoon into a deep serving bowl. Serve warm.

Note: To keep warm, place sauce bowl over a pan of hot water, and stir often. Cover closely with plastic wrap to prevent sauce from forming a skin.

Serves 8

Elder

SAMBUCUS NIGRA, ELDERBERRY

Strictly, elder is not a herb but a tall deciduous shrub which sends up many suckers from the root. Usually about 3 m high, it can reach as much as 10 m. It is included in herbals because it has a long history of medicinal and culinary uses. It was known to the Greeks and Romans and is common in European folklore.

Beautiful golden-leafed and variegated varieties are available. Stems have a soft pith centre and leaves are divided into five toothed leaflets up to 13 cm long. The small flowers are white to cream, in flat clusters about 20 cm across, and are followed by shiny purple-black berries. Fruit-set is usually sparse in hotter areas.

All parts of the plant, bark, leaves, flowers and fruit, have been used medicinally from time immemorial. Fruits are used in wine, jellies and jams. Flowers are used in fritters. The plant is still recommended for medical uses.

ELDER IN BLOOM

GROWING Grow elder in sun or semi-shade. The golden variety, grown for its leaf-colour, should be in full sun. A fertile loam that is damp but not badly drained is

DRIED ELDER FLOWERS

dolomite on acid soils to give a pH 6.0 to 8.0. A rich moist soil should produce usable roots in two to three years. Plant in back-row positions because of size. A high phosphorus, low nitrogen fertiliser can be used as a side-dressing. Elecampane is extremely hardy.

Seeds germinate easily and are sown in autumn for planting out in spring. Use a frame in cold areas. Offsets from the old root that have a bud can be taken in autumn, or roots can be cut into 5 to 6 cm pieces and struck in a rich, light, sandy soil in warm areas. A hot frame would be needed in the cold winter regions.

best. In acid soils lime or dolomite will be needed — from 120 g per square metre — to produce a pH 6.0 to 8.0. Elder is hardy and tolerates cold winter conditions.

No special care is required. Berry clusters are picked as required and the berries stripped from their stalks.

Elder can be raised from seed, but hardwood cuttings in spring or autumn strike very easily. Rooted pieces can be detached, or plants divided.

Elecampane

INULA HELENIUM, VELVET DOCK, WILD SUNFLOWER

This is a large, handsome perennial growing to 2 m high, with hairy, furrowed stems and large, golden daisy flowers. The roots are large, fleshy and branching, and produce a basal rosette of huge leaves 40 to 80 cm long on 30 cm stalks. Flowering stems then arise with stem-clasping leaves. The yellow daisy flowers are 7 cm across with straggly ray florets.

The roots of elecampane were used for candying and flavouring sweets. The whole plant is aromatic and was grown for use in country medicines.

GROWING Plants grow in shade, semi-shade and full sun but may not flower as well in the shade. A well-drained, moist, deep loamy soil is best. Incorporate lime or

ELECAMPANE BELONGS TO THE DAISY FAMILY

Evening Primrose

OENOTHERA BIENNIS (FAM. ONAGRACEAE)

The common name, evening primrose, refers mainly to *O. biennis* , which is an evening-flowering biennial that grows to 1 m or more and bears fragrant, yellow flowers.

GROWING Oenotheras will grow well in all garden soils, but prefer to be planted in a sunny position. Most species grow from seed while the perennial species are propagated by cuttings. Evening primrose will grow in most conditions except hot subtropical and tropical areas.

EVENING PRIMROSE (OENOTHERA BIENNIS)

Fennel

**FOENICULUM VULGARE SUBSP.
VULGARIS, WILD FENNEL,
F.V. VAR. AZORICUM, FLORENCE
FENNEL,
FINOCCHIO, F.V. VAR. DULCE,
SWEET FENNEL**

Florence fennel grows to about 1 m and often is annual in its growth, but may last into the second year or longer. It is distinguished by its bulb-like, thickened leaf bases.

Sweet fennel does not have the thickened leaf bases of Florence fennel, and is taller, growing up to 150 cm.

The fennels have lacy, divided, thread-like leaflets. Flowers in 10 to 15 rayed umbels are small and yellow. Fruits are about 6 to 8 cm long and are ribbed and brown in colour.

Uses of fennel are many with leaves chopped for fish, pork, veal. Seeds are used in herb vinegar, in biscuits and there are medicinal uses.

GROWING Full sun is best for both varieties. Although the fennels will grow in almost any soil, the best plants are grown in a well-drained loam enriched with manure or compost. Acid soils need ground limestone or dolomite to give a pH around pH 6.0 to 7.0. Fennels are hardy and roots survive winter, but in cold areas the plants should be cut back to about 10 cm from the ground in early winter.

There is some confusion of names in the types of fennel grown. Wild fennel has been declared a noxious weed in parts of New Zealand, South Australia, Victoria and Tasmania.

Fennels need only average care. Do not overwater. Harvest leaves before the flowers open. Seeds are harvested when the colour is greyish-green. If left too long they will drop and self-sow. Plant as a back-row plant. Heap up soil to blanch Florence fennel when the leaf bases start to swell.

Fennels self-sow easily. Sow seed in spring or autumn in drills 5 cm deep and 40 cm apart. Sow in spring only in cold areas. Root cuttings can be used 8 to 10 cm long.

Fenugreek

**TRIGONELLA FOENUMGRAECUM,
BIRD'S FOOT**

Fenugreek is a hardy annual and has slender stalks bearing three leaves and fragrant, cream flowers followed by long, slender seed pods.

This herb has assumed recent importance as its seeds have been discovered to contain diosgenin, an important chemical in oral contraceptives. Fenugreek leaves may also be dried and used as an ingredient in curries and the seeds are sometimes used in making chutney.

GROWING Fenugreek prefers a mild climate and well drained soil. Propagate by seed and allow 16 weeks for the plants to mature. Fenugreek grows well in a wide moisture and temperature range.

FENNEL (FOENICULUM VULGARE)

**FENNEL (FOENICULUM VULGARE)
IN FLOWER**

Foxglove

DIGITALIS PURPUREA, WITCHES' GLOVES, FAIRY'S GLOVE (AND MANY MORE)

Foxglove is a biennial, sometimes perennial, forming a rosette of large, downy leaves to 30 cm long from which 120 to 150 cm flowering stems emerge in the second summer. Flowers are tubular bells, 4 to 6 cm long, purple to crimson in colour, and there are many colourful varieties.

Foxgloves are lovely border plants. However, plants are poisonous, but drugs obtained commercially from the leaves and seeds are used in some heart conditions.

GROWING Foxgloves are usually grown in full sun, but some growers recommend some shade and plants in Europe grow in open places in woodland. An average garden loam will do, but for best results dig in organic matter and see that the soil does not dry out in summer. Lime or dolomite is essential on acid soils as foxgloves prefer pH 6.0 to 8.0. Use 200 to 300 g per square metre of ground limestone or dolomite, working it into the top 10 to 15 cm of soil at the first digging. Mulch plants in summer, and in late winter apply a heavy dressing of animal manure or compost, supplemented with a general fertiliser if necessary.

Foxgloves are sown in spring after the frost danger is past, although the roots stand many degrees of frost during the winter. The fine seed is best mixed with dry sand for sowing and plants can be transplanted 15 to 20 cm apart when large enough to handle, preferably during damp weather.

Garlic

ALLIUM SATIVUM, POOR MAN'S TREACLE

Garlic is a bulbous perennial with flat, green leaves growing 60 to 90 cm tall. The plants grow a flowering head enclosed in a papery sheath and develop tiny topset bulblets following off-white or purple tinged flowers. The bulbs have many crescent-shaped bulblets or cloves inside a papery sheath.

Because they are strongly pungent, garlic cloves are used sparingly. Cloves steeped in vinegar will give garlic vinegar. Garlic butter for hot rolls or bread is popular. There are still many who value garlic medicinally.

GROWING Garlic needs full sun. Soil should be well dug sandy loam with a ration of compost or cool animal manure. It should be moist and well drained, with a pH 5.5 to 6.7. Lime would be necessary only on strongly acid soils, 100 to 200 g of ground limestone or dolomite could be added per square metre. Garlic is hardy and can be planted in mid-winter. Keep weed free and damp but not overwet.

When leaves wither the whole plant is dug up. The dry leaves can be plaited and the plants hung up in an airy shed to dry.

Garlic is grown from the cloves. These are removed from the outer skin and separated. Small cloves can be used for cooking; the larger cloves, usually on the outside, are planted 5 cm deep, 20 cm apart in rows 30 cm apart. Sow by mid-winter, earlier in warm areas and in spring in very cold areas.

FOXGLOVE (*DIGITALIS PURPUREA*)

Above ◆ **GARLIC BULBS AND CLOVES (*ALLIUM SATIVUM*)**
Right ◆ **CRUNCHY VEGETABLES WITH GARLIC DIP**

CRUNCHY VEGETABLES WITH GARLIC DIP

1 bulb garlic, peeled
salt
8 thick slices stale white bread,
crusts removed
4 to 6 tablespoons lemon juice
1½ cups (375 ml) olive oil

Pureé garlic in a food processor with a good pinch salt.

Soak bread briefly in cold water, squeeze well to remove excess water and add bread to garlic with half the lemon juice. Process until smooth.

With the motor still running, add oil in a slow, steady stream until a thick white paste has formed. Adjust seasoning, adding more lemon juice to taste if necessary.

Makes 3 cups (750 ml)

Ginger

ZINGIBER OFFICINALE

Ginger is a rhizomatous perennial (rhizomes are creeping, underground stems) growing about 60 cm high with large, oblong leaves to 18 cm long, 2 cm wide. The flowers, which are yellow-green with a purple lip with cream markings, appear in dense spikes about 8 cm long.

Ginger is candied, preserved in syrup and widely used for flavouring cakes and biscuits. It is used in curry, pickles, chutney, meat sauces and cordials. It is also recommended for some stomach ailments.

DELICIOUS GINGER ROOT

GROWING Although many experts suggest a shady position to avoid sunburn of leaves, in Queensland ginger is grown in the open paddock and shaded only when necessary. A rich, well-drained loam, enriched with compost or animal manure is essential for good growth. The pH range should be suitable around pH 5.5 to 7.0, but some lime or dolomite, up to 300 g per square metre, would be advisable on very acid soils. Use a complete fertiliser like Tropic at 60 to 100 g per square metre, with monthly side-dressings of 10 g urea per square metre.

After planting, water the bed and cover with mulch of sawdust 7 to 8 cm deep. Dried

GINGER PLANTS

grass (not clippings), or straw can be up to 15 cm deep. Avoid overwatering, but keep soil damp. In hot, sunny weather, cover plants with 50 percent shade cloth to avoid heat sunburn. Harvest by mid-March to avoid too much fibre in the roots. Later harvested rhizomes can be dried and then ground.

Ginger is grown from pieces of rhizome planted in September with the top about 2 to 3 cm below the surface, spaced 15 to 20 cm apart in rows 45 cm apart.

Ginger grows outdoors in the tropics where temperatures during the season are above 15°C, but in cool or temperate regions it must be grown in a warm glasshouse. Indoors or under glass, it makes a good pot plant.

INGREDIENTS FOR HOT MANGO AND TOMATO CHUTNEY

Horehound

MARRUBIUM VULGARE, COMMON OR WHITE HOREHOUND

Horehound is a widespread perennial herb (declared a noxious weed in South Australia and Victoria) growing to about 45 cm high with wrinkled, grey to white woolly leaves, oval in shape and up to 5 cm long. The white flowers are small and clustered in the upper leaf axils.

Horehound is used for horehound ale and, medicinally, for a tea said to remedy coughs and colds.

GROWING Horehound is not fussy and grows in dry, open sunny situations or in part shade. Almost any soil will serve, but the plant seems to flourish in drier, poorer soils.

HOT MANGO AND TOMATO CHUTNEY

4 medium firm under-ripe mangoes, peeled, seeded and diced
6 under-ripe tomatoes, sliced
1 cm piece ginger root, finely grated
2 cloves garlic, minced
2 onions, chopped
1 cup (150 g) currants
4 red chillies, seeded and sliced
2 tablespoons chopped fresh coriander
¼ teaspoon cayenne pepper
2 cups (500 ml) malt vinegar
2 cups (350 g) brown sugar
salt

Place all ingredients in a heavy-based saucepan. Mix well and bring to boil, then simmer gently for 10 minutes. Reduce heat to low and cook, stirring until mangoes are soft, and mixture is a jam-like consistency. Add salt to taste.

Remove from heat and cool slightly. Bottle chutney in sterilised jars. Remove any air bubbles by piercing mixture with a skewer.

Cut out circles of greaseproof paper according to jar size. Place these on top of the chutney and press lightly with fingertips to remove air. Seal with sterilised lids. Store in a cool place and refrigerate after opening.

Makes 7 cups (1750 ml)

HOREHOUND IS AN EASY HERB TO GROW AND IS INVASIVE IN SOME AREAS

Horseradish

ARMORACIA RUSTICANA SYN. COCHLEARIA ARMORACIA, MOUNTAIN RADISH

Horseradish is a perennial herb with large, crinkly, lower leaves, up to 40 cm long and 23 cm wide, and smaller dock-like leaves higher on the 45 cm stem. Small white flowers appear in panicles on branching side stalks.

Horseradish root is used for the famous horseradish sauce and in other sauces, or as a condiment for meat and fish. The root is scrubbed, peeled and grated. Young leaves can be chopped for salad. It is thought to be an appetite stimulant, an aid to digestion, a diuretic and tonic.

GROWING An open sunny position is best, with deeply dug, fertile soil limed with ground limestone or dolomite, pH 6.0 to 7.0 is ideal. The lime can be broadcast at the rate of 200 to 300 g per square metre. A week later dig in a heavy dressing of animal manure. Drainage must be good. Horseradish will tolerate heavy frosts. Although perennial, horseradish can be lifted every year or two, the small roots used and the main roots replanted each spring.

Although horseradish can be raised from cuttings, better and earlier plants are grown from pieces of root 1 to 2 cm thick and 20 to 22 cm long, from which side roots have been removed. Each piece of root should have a small piece of crown or a growing point, although any piece of root will grow. Planting holes should be 30 to 40 cm deep, made with a dibber. Space them 30 to 45 cm apart. Fill with fine soil after planting. Allow only two or three shoots to grow on each plant.

FRESH HORSERADISH

6 tablespoons grated horseradish roots
2 teaspoons salt
2 tablespoons raw sugar
¼ cup (60 ml) vinegar

Wash roots and peel. Place in a food processor and blend until finely chopped. Add salt, sugar and vinegar to taste. Alternatively, grate roots into a small bowl and stir in salt, sugar and vinegar to taste. Pack into sterilised jars and refrigerate until required. Tastes delicious served with roast beef, oily fish and grilled steak.

Makes 200 ml

HORSERADISH, SHOWING THE ROOT OF THE PLANT

HORSERADISH (COCHLEARIA ARMORACIA)

Hyssop

HYSSOPUS OFFICINALIS

Hyssop is a compact but shrubby perennial growing 45 to 60 cm high with glossy, dark green leaves and small, decorative, white, pink or blue flowers, suitable for cutting. The leaves have a pungent aroma.

A bit too spicy for modern taste, hyssop can be tried in soups, stews, salads, stuffings. It is added to some liqueurs and perfumes and a tea is made for medicinal use. It can be put in pot-pourri and is recommended as a companion plant for grape vines to increase yield.

GROWING Hyssop needs full sun and a light, well-drained loam, about pH 6.0; lime or dolomite should be added at about 200 g per square metre if the soil is acid. Hyssop stands a cold climate with temperatures as low as -38°C.

Minimal care is needed for the plants, usually only weeding and watering. Trimming after flowering and in late winter will help to keep the plants from becoming straggly. In late winter a side dressing of manure plus a little sprinkling of mixed fertiliser will start the new growth.

Raise hyssop from seed sown in damp soil in September, or you can strike some cuttings or grow plants from division of roots. Space plants about 30 cm apart.

Above ◆ **LAVENDER FLOWERS**
Left ◆ **LAVENDER FIELDS**

Lavender

**LAVANDULA ANGUSTIFOLIA,
ENGLISH LAVENDER,
L. DENTATA, FRENCH
LAVENDER,
L. STOECHAS, SPANISH
LAVENDER**

The lavenders are mostly shrubby perennials growing from about 30 to 90 cm high or a little more. English lavender has whitish leaves when young becoming green later. French lavender has marginally toothed leaves that are densely woolly and grey to silvery grey. Spanish lavender, also sometimes listed as French or Italian lavender, is more bushy and spreading but will reach 90 to 100 cm and leaves tend to be more green-grey than silver-grey with dark purple, somewhat cone-like flowers, with a tuft or purple bracts at the tip.

English and Spanish lavenders are the types grown for their fragrance in perfumery. There are many other cultivars and a few other varieties. Most of the cultivars belong to *Lavandula angustifolia*, subspecies *angustifolia* (syn. *L. officinalis, L. spica, L. vera and L. delphinensis)*, such as 'Alba', white lavender, 'Rosea', pink lavender, and 'Nana', dwarf lavender. The various names of lavender are

MAKE YOUR OWN LAVENDER WATER, USING THE EASY RECIPE IN THE BOX BELOW

years old tend to be straggly and unthrifty and should be replaced then by young plants from cuttings or layers.

Lavenders can be grown from seed, but some varieties do not germinate well whereas cuttings strike readily. Take side pieces with a heel, or tips, and plant firmly in damp sand. When new growth is evident the cuttings are planted out, spacing them 50 to 60 cm apart. In plantations for oil production, the young cuttings are spaced 45 cm apart each way and in the second spring every alternate plant is removed, leaving the mature bushes 90 cm apart.

Sometimes older plants of *Lavandula angustifolia* can be divided. All lavenders can be layered by pegging down suitable low-placed side branches.

confused but 'Vera' for L. vera is a form sometimes called Dutch lavender.

The main use for lavender is for fragrance in sachets and perfumes. It may be some use also as a moth repellent. Flowers can be candied and can be used to make a lavender vinegar.
GROWING Give lavenders full sun. The essential is a well-drained soil, preferably a crumbly, sandy loam. Too much water in winter is not desirable, while a soil that is over-rich is said to reduce oil yield and produce excessive leaf growth. Acid soils will require ground limestone or dolomite for a pH range of pH 6.5 to 7.5. Dressings of 200 to 300 g per square metre may be needed at the first digging and should be renewed every second or third year. A

mixed fertiliser with a high phosphorus, high potash ratio has been shown overseas to be useful for high oil production and additional fragrance in the flowers. A ratio of 5% nitrogen, 6% phosphorus and 7% potassium would be satisfactory. To make 5 kg of mixture, mix 1.2 kg sulphate of ammonia, 2.6 kg superphosphate and 900 g of sulphate of potash. To this add 300 g of dolomite as a filler to make up to the 5 kg. Use this mixture at 30 to 60 g per plant.

The lavenders are fairly hardy and most species will stand heavy frost especially if mulched in winter. A frost of -18°C is not too cold, but French lavender is more tender and should have protection from temperatures below -9°C. Do not allow plants to flower too young. Plants over five

Uses of Lavender

Lavenders all originate from mountainous areas of the Mediterranean. They all have silvery grey leaves which can be clipped to form a low hedge, as they were in Tudor knot gardens.

Lavender has been widely used for cooking and in medicine in the past, but these days its aromatic leaves and flowers are mostly used in cosmetics. It is ideal for pot-pourri and can help repel moths in linen, carpets and clothes, wardrobes and chests.

Lavender oil is a distillation of French lavender flowers and leaves. Creams using this oil can relieve muscular stiffnes and a cold compress applied to the forehead will temper a headache or giddiness.

Lavender water can be made by dropping a few drops of lavender oil into 600 ml chemist's alcohol with a lump of sugar. Shake well and transfer to an attractive bottle.

Lemon Grass

CYMBOPOGON CITRATUS, FAM. GRAMINEAE

One of about 40 species of perennial tropical grasses, this plant is often cultivated for its aromatic oil which is used in perfumery. It is found wild in southern India and Ceylon.

Lemon grass forms dense clumps or tufts to almost 2 m high. The leaves are almost 1 m long and 17 cm wide and the branches are slender and nodding at ends. The foliage is highly scented.

It is a popular herb in Thai cooking and gives a wonderful lemon flavour to many dishes.

Lemon grass contains Vitamin A and is frequently used in skin cosmetics. Chop fresh leaves into the teapot to make a healthy infusion for healthy eyes and skin.

GROWING Lemon grass appreciates copious watering, full sun and rich soil. Propagation is by division. Divide clumps and relocate. Lemon grass can be grown in subtropical and tropical regions of Australia. It grows in a climate of wet subtropics to tropical coast.

Right ◆ **LEMON VERBENA LIKES MILD CONDITIONS**
Below ◆ **LEMON GRASS (CYMBOPOGON CITRATUS)**

Lemon Verbena

ALOYSIA TRIPHYLLA, SYNS. LIPPIA CITRIODORA, ALOYSIA CITRIODORA

Lemon verbena is not a herb, strictly, but a tall deciduous shrub to 3 m high or even more. The narrow leaves are in whorls of three or four. The leaves are 8 cm long, with a strong lemon fragrance. Flowers vary from white to mauve in clusters 10 to 20 cm long.

The leaves retain their lemon fragrance for months, even years and are used in potpourri and sachets and for flavouring or making a fragrant tea.

GROWING A warm, full-sun, sheltered position is best, with an average, well-drained loam, not over-rich in manure.

Strongly acid soils should be dressed with ground limestone or dolomite to give pH 6.0 to 8.0. Although of tropical origin, lemon verbena will stand some frost and has survived -12°C, but it is wise to mulch plants in cold weather. Where winters are extreme, plants can be grown in containers and brought under cover before cold weather arrives.

Young plants should be pinched, and given light pruning in the first winter. Heavier pruning is needed in subsequent winters to keep lemon verbena from getting too straggly. Usual average garden care is all that is necessary.

Lemon verbena can be raised from hardwood cuttings in the open ground in winter, or by half-ripe cuttings in early autumn. Seeds can be sown, but can be difficult to germinate.

Lovage

LEVISTICUM OFFICINALE SYN. LEGUSTICUM OFFICINALIS

This is a strikingly ornamental perennial herb to 180 cm high. The root is a 15 cm taproot like a carrot. The basal leaves are rather like celery and a dark glossy green. The flowers, on long dividing stems, are yellow to green yellow in flattened umbels. The seeds are yellowish brown with winged ribs.

As lovage is powerfully aromatic, only small amounts are used. It is used in soups, stews and white sauces. Small amounts of leaf chopped up are used in salads and blanched stalks can be cooked with vegetables. Medical uses have been recommended, and the herb is used for a tea.

GROWING Lovage can be grown in full sun or partial shade, but is not suitable for hot areas. For lovage prepare a well-drained, rich, moist soil that is basically a light, friable loam allowing easy root penetration. As a slightly alkaline soil is best, pH 6.5 to 7.6, lime or dolomite should be dug into acid soils initially. Dig deeply, but mix the lime in the top 10 to 15 cm. Heavy ration of organic matter, animal manure and/or compost should be dug in later. Lovage is hardy and will tolerate temperatures as low as -21°C.

Keep the soil free of weeds. In dry summer areas a mulch keeps the soil cooler. Regular watering is essential. Leaves and stalks can be picked regularly, but avoid removing the central stem.

Seed is exceptionally easy to germinate, but should be sown as soon as it is ripe, usually in late summer. Seedlings can be transplanted 30 cm apart each way in autumn or early spring. Root division can be used if each piece has a growing eye.

Marigold

CALENDULA OFFICINALIS, CALENDULA, POT MARIGOLD

Marigold is a much branched annual herb to about 60 cm high or more. The pale green, oblong-oval leaves are about 5 to 15 cm long and flowers vary from 4 to 10 cm across. While the species is a single orange flower, cultivars vary from pale yellow to deep orange and some have double flowers.

The single flowered marigold is favoured; the strap-like ray florets round the outside of the flower are used. The crushed flower petals are added to soups, stews, cheese, scrambled eggs, mayonnaise and salads, and the yellow colouring is a substitute for saffron.

Oils, ointments and infusions of the petals have been used medicinally. Marigold tea can be made.

POT MARIGOLD (CALENDULA OFFICINALIS)

GROWING Give pot marigolds full sun and an average garden soil. Pot marigolds, or calendulas, are exceptionally easy to germinate and grow. Very acid soils will need liming, plants favour neutral soil, around pH 6.0 to 8.0. At the initial digging

LOVAGE THRIVES IN DAMP RICH CONDITIONS

MARIGOLDS (CALENDULA OFFICINALIS)

Marjoram

ORIGANUM MAJORANA, SYN. MAJORANA HORTENSIS, SWEET, ANNUAL OR KNOTTED MARJORAM

Marjoram is a perennial herb about 30 to 60 cm high. It is sometimes grown as an annual because it may die out in cold, wet winters. The leaves are rounded to oval and vary from less than a centimetre to over 2 cm long. The tiny flowers in small spikelets about 2 cm long are white, or tinged purple or pink. Leaves are fragrant.

Marjoram is used freely to season soups, cheese dishes, and in omelettes, salads, and meat and poultry stuffings. It is also excellent with Italian dishes - tomato sauces, pasta and pizza and goes well with potatoes and rice.

It also has medicinal properties. It is used to strengthen and condition the hair and its oil, rubbed into aching joints and muscles, relieves stiffness. Marjoram has remarkable antiseptic qualities. A regular intake is said to cleanse the blood and keep you free of stomach bugs. If you have a toothache, chew a few leaves.

GROWING Marjoram needs full sun and a moderately rich, well-drained loam. Additions of compost or well-rotted animal

apply ground limestone or dolomite at 120 to 600 g per square metre. Some organic matter such as compost or animal manure can be incorporated a few days before planting. This helps to retain moisture for marigolds must not be allowed to dry out. Pot marigolds are very hardy, although heavy frosts will kill the flowers.

Pot marigolds require no special care, other than dead-heading to prolong blooming, and water in hot, dry weather. Watch for calendula rust, the reddish fungus on the leaves and spray immediately, or pull up and burn badly affected plants.

Pot marigolds are raised from seed which is sown thinly in boxes or seed beds from January to May in temperate areas, from September to January in cold areas, and from March to June in hot areas. Sow seed 1 cm deep. Seedlings should emerge in about two to three weeks. Allow the plants to grow to about 4 cm high before transplanting. Seed can also be sown direct into rows about 30 cm apart.

MARJORAM (ORIGANUM MAJORANA)

manure help to retain moisture. Marjoram must not be allowed to dry out, so give the plant adequate water. Although some writers have suggested an acidic soil, American research seems to show a pH around the neutral point, pH 6.0 to 8.0 is needed. Strongly acid soils should therefore have dressings of lime or dolomite.

Sweet marjoram is somewhat tender and in frost areas must be raised in the spring after frost danger is over. Plants can be pot-grown in cold areas. Keep up the water supply, and if unexpected cold weather is experienced, cover plants with cloches, or some protection.

Leaves are picked just as the flowers are starting to open and can be dried by suspending them in paper bags in a dry, airy room, preferably with a temperature not above 23°C.

Marjoram is usually raised from seed sown in spring. As the seed is small, mix it with fine dry sand and broadcast it thinly over the seedbox soil. Press into the surface. Seedlings can be moved to pots when the first four leaves have developed. When plants have plenty of root, transplant 25 cm apart. Marjoram will also strike from small cuttings in spring or autumn. A warm frame will be needed for autumn cuttings in cold areas. Layers of side branches also strike readily and older bushes can be divided and replanted.

MARJORAM IN FLOWER

Mint

MENTHA X PIPERITA, PEPPERMINT
M. X PIPERITA VAR. *CITRATA*, EAU-DE-COLOGNE, BERGAMOT OR LEMON MINT
M. SUAVEOLENS, APPLE MINT, CV. 'VARIEGATA', PINEAPPLE MINT
M. PULEGIUM, PENNYROYAL
M. SPICATA SYN. *M. VIRIDIS*, SPEARMINT

There are hundreds of species of mint named, but as mint hybridises readily these are thought to be forms or hybrids of about two dozen or so species. All the mints are perennials, either upright or prostrate growing. Stems are mostly square in cross-section. Because stems take root readily in the soil and propagate also by runners, plants may become invasive. In height they vary from as low as 3 cm to taller kinds from 20 to 90 cm or more. Leaves vary from narrow and pointed shape to rounded and oval shape. Flowers are usually white, pink, lilac or purple.

Mints are well-known for flavourings, as condiments, as a tea, and for use in salads, sandwiches, sauces, with peas etc. Menthol is extracted commercially from some varieties such as Corsican mint, *M. requieni*, and has medical uses.

GROWING A warm, sunny aspect suits the mints, but in full sun they must not be allowed to dry out.

Mint does best in a moist, moderately rich soil, pH around neutral point, that is, pH 6.0 to 8.0. Most mints are extremely hardy tolerating frosts to -29°C, but pennyroyal and Corsican mint, *Mentha requieni*, are tender below -15°C.

Mints are easy to grow although they are attacked by caterpillars, snails and slugs, and (except for a variety, *Mentha rubra var. raripila*) are susceptible to rust. Infected plants should be burnt and burning straw, trash or paper on the bed has been recommended for destruction of rust spores. Replanting healthy young runners in a new bed will eliminate rust. It has been suggested that a lime dressing, if the soil is acid, may be of some use in inhibiting rust. Removal of old stems may also help.

The ground should be enclosed by slates, fibro or deep concrete edges — 30 to 40 cm deep — to prevent mint spreading

Above ◆ **PEPPERMINT (*MENTHA PIPERITA*)**
Below ◆ **SPEARMINT (*MENTHA SPICATA*)**

where it is not wanted. Alternatively grow mint in planter boxes, or a large tub or trough near the kitchen door.

Mint can be raised easily from seeds when available, but is so easy from divisions or runners that these are usually used. It is an advantage to start a new bed in a new position about every third year.

Which mint?

With over 40 varieties of mint to choose from, enthusiastic cooks may well wonder which mint to choose. Generally mint recipes use applemint or peppermint, but all mints go well with lamb, vegetables, fruit and cool drinks. However, part of the joy of herbs is discovering new taste combinations and flavours, so experiment until you find the mint you prefer.

Applemint exudes a powerful apple fragrance and flavour.

Spearmint makes a refreshing tea and aids digestion, dispelling flatulence, as does peppermint tea, which also improves the appetite and is a general good tonic.

Mustard

BRASSICA NIGRA SYN. SINAPIS NIGRA, BLACK MUSTARD, BRASSICA HIRTA SYN. SINAPIS ALBA, WHITE MUSTARD

The mustards are annual herbs. Black mustard varies in height from 90 to 180 cm and is freely branching. White mustard grows from 30 to 90 cm high and is more erect. Leaves of the white mustard are divided, oval in outline and about 2 cm long. Those of black mustard are pinnatifid. Both have typical yellow crucifer flowers. Seeds of white mustard are pale yellow to white in hairy pods; those of the black mustard reddish-brown. Good mustard is a mixture of the powdered white and black seeds, the latter being more pungent.

White mustard is the one usually grown with cress. Mustard leaves are used in salads and even the pungent older leaves have culinary potential. Mustard has medicinal uses in poultices and baths to relieve soreness.

GROWING Both mustards prefer a sunny position. Where grown for seed, average soils will suit, but the white mustard does best on a clay loam and black mustard on a sandy loam. White mustard should not be too damp, black mustard likes plenty of moisture. Lime is advisable on acid soils for a range of pH 6.0 to 7.5.

Mustard is usually sown in the spring out of doors; when grown inside with cress frosts are no problem. In cold areas, seed can be grown under a cloche except in very heavy frost, where it would fail. Give plants normal garden care.

Flowering heads are picked before the seed is fully ripe so that it is not lost by scattering. They are then dried and threshed for seed.

Right ◆ **A GOLDEN FIELD OF MUSTARD**

Mustards are grown from seed. If growing black and white mustard, the black is usually sown one or two weeks earlier than the white. Broadcast, or sow in drills 30 to 60 cm apart.

As a rule white mustard is germinated in small pans or trays with cress (Lepidium sativum) and is sown four days later than the cress. A light sandy soil is used with some powdered charcoal added to keep the soil sweet. Water only to keep the soil damp, not wet. The tender young leaves are cut for sandwiches or salads when about 3 cm high. Successive sowings are needed for a continuous supply.

Nasturtium

TROPAEOLUM MAJUS, INDIAN CRESS
TROPAEOLUM MINUS, DWARF NASTURTIUM

Nasturtiums are the well known, gaily coloured flowering plants. Dwarf nasturtiums grow to about 40 cm high while the trailing, tall nasturtiums have stems 180 to 200 cm long and can climb supports with their twining leaf stalks. The leaves are almost circular with veins radiating from a near-central leaf stalk. The flowers are bright yellow, orange or red to deep maroon and are spurred. Seeds are carried in a rounded, ridged, three-chambered fruit.

Nasturtium flower buds and fruits are both pickled in a similar way to capers. Some double flowers do not set seed, so if fruits are wanted, plants with single flowers should be sown. Flowers and leaves are used in salads. All parts of the plant are edible and have a peppery mustard oil that is piquant.

GROWING Although nasturtiums like full sun, they can tolerate part shade as is shown by the dwarf plants, which make colourful indoor plants if given a well-lit spot. Any average garden soil will suit nasturtiums. If grown for flowers and fruit, a not too rich, well-drained, sandy soil on the dry side is ideal, but for leaves for salads it is better to use an organic-matter enriched soil. Plants need good drainage. Lime, ground limestone or dolomite, will be needed on acid soils to produce more neutral conditions, pH 6.0 to 8.0. Work in lime a couple of weeks before sowing at from 200 to 500 g per square metre according to soil acidity.

Nasturtiums are frequently treated as annuals, particularly in cooler areas, where they are sown from spring to mid-summer. In milder areas they are quite hardy. Flowering is over a long period so regular picking of the fruits for pickling is necessary.

Seed is sown September to December in cold areas, and also in August, January and February in mild areas. In warm areas sow from February to September. Seeds can be sown in clumps of 3 or 4 seeds, with 30 cm between the clumps, or for trailing nasturtiums, sow 2 or 3 seeds 75 cm apart. Water moderately until germinated.

STUFFED NASTURTIUM LEAVES

*24 to 30 nasturtium leaves,
very well washed
1 quantity Herbed Cream Cheese
paprika to taste
nasturtium flowers, to garnish*

Herbed Cream Cheese
*1 cup (250 g) creamed cottage cheese or
farm cheese
1 clove garlic, crushed with a pinch salt
freshly ground black pepper
juice ½ lemon
6 tablespoons chopped fresh herbs, such as
parsley, basil, oregano
¼ bunch chives, snipped*

Shake the leaves dry. Spread a thick layer of herb cheese over one half of each leaf. Fold the other half of the leaf over and press lightly to seal. Do not completely close. Lightly sprinkle exposed cheese with paprika. Chill and serve garnished with nasturtium flowers.

To prepare Herbed Cream Cheese: In a bowl combine cottage cheese, garlic, pepper, lemon juice and herbs.

Serves 6 to 8

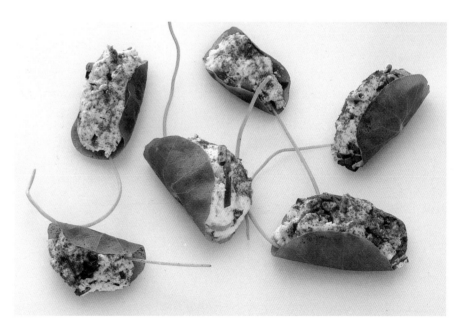

Above ◆ **NASTURTIUMS
(TROPAEOLUM MAJUS)**
Right ◆ **STUFFED NASTURTIUM LEAVES**

Oregano

ORIGANUM VULGARE, WILD MARJORAM, OREGANO

Wild marjoram is a perennial growing to 75 cm in a mat-like, creeping fashion. Leaves are dark green, long oval to 4 cm, and smooth or hairy. Small clusters of purple flowers appear in late summer on erect stems about 45 cm high. You can grow your own oregano but the commercially bought kind may be made from more than one of the marjorams (*Origanum* species), or even from other plants such as *Coleus amboinicus*.

Oregano is an excellent, floriferous ground cover. It is also a pungent flavouring for meat dishes, fish, stews, gravies, aubergines and cheese. It is frequently used in Italian, Spanish and Mexican dishes.

GROWING A well-drained, not too rich soil is best in full sun. A heavy dressing of ground limestone or dolomite should be applied before planting; use 200 to 300 g of dolomite on acid soils. Wild marjoram stands temperatures down to -35°C so it is frost hardy. Don't allow plants to dry out.

Cut back flower stalks after flowering. Plants tend to become woody and need replacing about every third year.

Sow seed by sprinkling on top of a prepared seed bed or pan. Just firm the seed in and do not cover deeply. Spring sowing is best in cool areas. The prostrate branches layer themselves so that plants can be easily divided for further planting.

Above ◆ **OREGANO (*ORIGANUM VULGARE*)**
Below ◆ **OREGANO IS ONE OF THE HERBS USED IN *BOUQUET GARNI***

Orris

IRIS X GERMANICA VAR. FLORENTINA

Orris is the powdered, violet-scented rhizome of var. florentina of the much-grown garden irises. It is used in perfumery, and although it is the major source of orris, it is not the only source. Some other old world irises are sometimes used. It is a typical iris with the typical sword-shaped, flag-like leaves and beautiful flowers up to 60 cm tall.

The iris rhizomes are dried and ground and used in perfumes and pot-pourris as a fixative, and for their violet fragrance.

GROWING These iris do best in full sun. Give them a well-drained soil and avoid wet positions for they are then susceptible to rhizome rot. A light sandy soil is ideal, pH range around neutral point, pH 6.0 to 8.0. Acid soils should have 100 to 300 g of dolomite or ground limestone incorporated two or three weeks before planting. Some compost or manure, preferably kept away from the rhizome, plus a ration of complete fertiliser, if necessary, can also be added at planting time. Iris are hardy in all save the coldest areas. These iris are good performers and no trouble providing they are not planted where it is too wet.

Most usual propagation is by division of the rhizome as soon as flowering is over. Discard damaged or soft rhizomes and trim the leaves to a fan-shape about 12 to 15 cm or so above the rhizome. Plant with half the rhizome above the soil surface.

Ripe seed can be sown in pans or seed beds of light sandy soil. Use a frame in cold areas. When the seedlings are large enough to handle, they can be pricked out into boxes or individual pots to grow on for later planting out. Germination is often irregular and may take fifteen months or longer. For final plantings, space 30 cm apart or plant in informal clumps and irregular drifts.

Parsley

PETROSELINUM CRISPUM VAR. CRISPUM SYNS P. HORTENSE, P. SATIVUM, CARUM PETROSELINUM, P. CRISPUM VAR. NEAPOLITANUM, ITALIAN PARSLEY, P. CRISPUM VAR. TUBEROSUM, TURNIP-ROOTED OR HAMBURG PARSLEY

The typical curly parsley is more favoured than Italian parsley. The turnip-rooted parsley produces a root of delicate flavour. Culturally much the same treatment is given to these three types.

The well known curly variety of parsley grows to approximately 30 cm with flower stalks reaching up to 80 to 90 cm.

Italian parsley is similar except that the leaves are divided into three flat, broad, roughly triangular leaflets.

Turnip-rooted parsley has flat leaves like Italian parsley, but each of the three leaflets is deeply incised into four or five cut segments. The root is swollen, parsnip-like and edible.

Flowers of all three are green-white to green-yellow in compound umbels and sometimes tinged red. The tall, central flower stem is hollow and has smaller leaves.

Parsley is used in salads, as a garnish, or chopped in all sorts of dishes. Parsley tea and parsley jelly are made from dried or fresh leaves. Parsley is one of the herbs used in a bouquet garni.

GROWING Give sun or half-shade to all parsley. In the sun, more care is needed to keep soil moist. A moist, well-drained, moderately rich soil gives the best results. American tests report pH 5.0 to 7.0 (neutral point) and also pH 6.0 to 8.0 (alkaline) as optimum conditions. My own parsley flourishes in a soil that is not limed and has a reading of pH 6.0 so lime would seem to be necessary only in extremely acid soils. Parsley is hardy in all but the coldest areas where frames can be used in winter. The flat-leaf types are slightly more cold tolerant.

Above ◆ **CURLY PARSLEY (PETROSELINUM CRISPUM)**
Below ◆ **ITALIAN PARSLEY (PETROSELINUM NEAPOLITANUM)**

Turnip-rooted parsley needs a deeper bed, to about 25 cm deep, as for carrot or parsnip, and should have animal manure plus an occasional dusting of a complete low-nitrogen fertiliser. Parsley and Italian parsley can have nitrogenous manures or be fed with liquid manure.

When harvesting parsley, pick leaves from the outside of the plant because new growth takes place from the centre of the crown.

Parsley is grown from seed sown in spring (autumn and winter as well in warm areas). Although biennial it is usually sown afresh each year. In suitable conditions it will self-sow readily. Seeds are slow to germinate, taking from 2 to 8 weeks. To speed results seed can be soaked in warm water for about twenty-four hours before sowing.

Here is a very quick method for germinating seed. Wet a jute sack in a bucket of boiling water. Sprinkle seed immediately over one half of the sack and fold the other half over to cover the seed. Then roll up the sack and keep in a warm position. Usually root emergence will be starting in three days and the sprouting

seeds can be picked off the sack and sown in 2 cm drills, 3 to 4 cm apart in a box or seed-bed. Keep damp until the first leaf appears. Italian parsley usually germinates more easily in 3 to 4 days.

Transplant bought or self-raised seedlings into prepared beds, with organic-enriched soil, or into 20 to 25 cm pots for indoor growing. Space 20 to 30 cm apart for good results. Beds must not be allowed to dry out. Do not allow flower stalks to grow the first year, but pick them off as soon as they emerge in the middle of the plant.

Pepper

PIPER NIGRUM, BLACK OR WHITE PEPPER

Pepper is a smooth-leaved, stout climbing plant which may reach 6 m or more in height, but when cultivated is usually restricted to 3 or 4 m. The large leaves are elliptical to almost circular in shape and from 12 to 18 cm long and 5 to 10 cm wide. Tiny white flowers appear in hanging spikes about 15 to 18 cm long, followed by round, green berries, which turn red, then black with a roughly wrinkled surface. Sometimes vines have flowers of only one sex; sometimes vines are bisexual. Berries will not set on vines with male flowers. On those with female flowers, berries will set only if there are male flowers in the vicinity.

Pepper is well-known as a condiment but also has medicinal uses. **GROWING** Filtered sunlight is desirable for best results, and a rich, moist but not wet, well-drained soil. A fairly neutral soil, pH 6.0 to 7.5, is best, so that ground limestone or dolomite could be incorporated before planting in acid soils, with a side-dressing, repeated every second or third year.

Peppers are vines of the hot wet tropics and a minimum temperature needed would be 16°C.

For black pepper, the berries are picked when not fully ripe. Sun ripening turns them black. For white pepper, berries are picked when ripe and the hulls removed. The corms are dried and then ground. White pepper is milder. A form of white pepper is also made by stripping the black hulls from black pepper.

Pepper is propagated from half-ripe cuttings about 45 cm long from terminal parts of the vine. Usually two or three are planted at the foot of the tree or post that is to support them. They are taken only from vines that carry heavy crops of berries. As the life of a vine is about 15 years and plants take three or four years to come into bearing it is advisable to start new plants in the tenth or eleventh year of a vine.

Cuttings are set at the foot of trees such as coconut palms, erythrinas, or coffee trees. Posts can be used to support them. Thereafter regular top dressing and watering will keep the vines producing.

Pyrethrins

PYRETHRUM

Pyrethrum, containing insecticidally active pyrethrins, is extracted from the flowers of *Chrysanthemum cinerariaefolium* which is grown commercially for this purpose in Kenya, Ecuador, New Guinea and China. The dried flowers themselves contain between 1 and 3 percent pyrethrins and chemical extracts containing up to 60 percent pyrethrins are used for the manufacture of many aerosols used domestically against flying insects, such as flies and mosquitoes. They are considered amongst the safest of domestic sprays, being highly active as knock down sprays with no residual effect. To improve knock down effects, many products are activated by the addition of other chemicals. Some products are water based and can be used as floral and garden sprays. Pyrethrum garden sprays can be used for caterpillars, aphids, bugs, beetles, leafhoppers. Witholding period is one day.

Above ◆ **CHRYSANTHEMUM CINERARIAEFOLIUM**

Left ◆ **BLACK PEPPER**

Rosemary

ROSMARINUS OFFICINALIS, COMPASS PLANT

ROSEMARY (*ROSMARINUS OFFICINALIS*)

Strictly speaking, rosemary is not a herb, but a medium growing, woody shrub, 60 to 120 cm high and occasionally taller. Young shoots are hairy, and mature leaves are narrow and leathery, 2 to 4 cm long, dark green and glossy above and grey-green beneath. The leaves have a resinous, pine-like fragrance. Flowers are in clusters, small and pale blue, white or pink, some cultivars having brighter colours.

The fresh flowering tops are used in perfumery and medicine and, although producing inferior oil of rosemary, leaves and stems are also used. In the kitchen, rosemary is used to flavour meat dishes, for example, sprigs are placed on top of roast lamb. Chopped leaves are used in stews, soups and casseroles, with bland vegetables, in biscuits and bread-making and to flavour jellies, wines and liqueurs.

GROWING Give rosemary full sun and a well-drained, quite poor soil on the dry side. Plants are resilient, making excellent dwarf windbreaks for herb gardens, even those close to the sea. Widespread experience shows that lime is needed on acid soils, from 100 to 300 g of dolomite according to soil type. Gillian Painter, the Auckland herb grower, suggests crushing eggshells as a useful additive to neutralise acidity. M. Grieve, in *A Modern Herbal,* remarks that on chalk soil (that is, strongly alkaline soil, about pH 8.5) rosemary is dwarfer in growth but has greater fragrance. Rosemary is hardy to -18°C, that is, in all but the coldest areas, and in those areas it makes an excellent pot plant, if it can be brought indoors in the winter.

As rosemary is a slow starter, pinching out the tip may slow it even more, but will start side buds into growth. Thereafter pinch tip buds each spring and, if necessary, lightly trim after flowering to preserve a compact, neat bush. Over-watering and over-feeding should be avoided, but give sufficient water in hot, dry areas.

Rosemary is propagated from seed, cuttings, layers, and even sometimes by division of older plants. Seeds are slow to germinate. fifteen cm cuttings taken in February and potted firmly (10 cm covered) in coarse sand strike readily, so this is the most popular method. For layers, a low branch is pulled down to the earth and an incision made in the bark. The branch is then pegged down with a wire hook and covered with sand. Keep cuttings and layers damp but not wet, at all times.

Rue

RUTA GRAVEOLENS, HERB-OF-GRACE

This is a hardy, decorative evergreen sub-shrub with shiny blue-green leaves. It grows about 90 to 120 cm high. Leaves are deeply cut into blunt-ended, spatula-shaped segments and emit a strong odour often thought to be disagreeable. *R. graveolens* 'Variegata' has variegated leaves. Contact with the leaves can cause severe dermatitis. Flowers are yellow, appearing in loose corymbs in summer. The brown seed capsules have an attractive shape.

Rue is used little as a culinary herb because most people consider it has a nauseous taste. Sometimes a few chopped leaves are used in salads, and it does have some medical uses. If you are not allergic to it, rue makes a decorative small specimen plant, or hedge for the herb garden.

RUE IN FLOWER

GROWING Rue needs full sun or semi-shade and will tolerate the poorest soils. Grown in good soils, it seems less frost resistant, but normally will tolerate temperatures to -29°C. It does best in well-drained, gravelly, or coarse sandy soils. Probably a soil with a pH 6.0 to 7.0 would be best, which means acid soils would need liming with 100 to 300 g of dolomite. The herb required little care. Shorten in spring to keep the bush compact and shapely.

Seed is sown in spring in beds or pans and thinned when 5 cm high. A week or two later transplant 45 cm apart. Cuttings or rooted side-pieces strike easily when planted in sandy soil in spring.

Saffron

CROCUS SATIVUS

Saffron is a low growing plant with narrow, grass-like leaves and a somewhat flattened but rounded corm. The overall height with the flower-spike of typical crocus flowers is about 45 cm. (The plant must not be confused with the thistle-like safflower.) The leaves are deeply ribbed and the flowers lilac-coloured with bright yellow or orange-red stigmas from which saffron dye is obtained.

Saffron was used for food colouring, but has been largely superseded because of the high cost of collecting and processing it. It also has medicinal uses.

GROWING Saffron will grow in semi-shade but does best in full sun. The soil must be well-drained, and for preference should be a light sandy loam. A pH 6.0 to 8.0 gives best results, therefore acid soils require dressing with ground limestone or dolomite. For strongly acid soils use up to 400 g per square metre and work thoroughly into the top 15 cm of soil at least two weeks before planting. Incorporate organic matter such as leafmould or ripe compost. Saffron crocuses stand heavy frosts and in fact are only suitable for growing in cold, winter areas.

Beds should be well dug and the soil friable. Plants can remain in place for three or four years before lifting. They flower in autumn and stigmas are picked out by hand and dried in the sun or on wire-gauze trays over a low heat. When dry they are immediately stored in air-tight, screw-top bottles in a dark cupboard because light will bleach them.

Corms are planted in January in rows 15 cm apart, allowing 8 to 10 cm between corms and setting them in a pocket of sand from 5 to 8 cm deep. Seeds are also used, but as three to four years are needed to reach flowering stage, corms are usually preferred.

Sage

SALVIA OFFICINALIS

Sage is a perennial semi-woody sub-shrub growing about 50 to 60 cm high or more, with rough-textured grey-green leaves from 3 to 6 cm long. Young stems are generally white-woolly. Blue, white or pink flowers are in vertical, spike-like clusters.

Sage is much used in cooking with meat, fish, pork and poultry. It was used for centuries to flavour sausages and, with thyme and onion, is made into stuffing for meat-rolls and poultry. It has many other culinary uses, and is used for a herb tea, medicines, and as a shampoo.

SAGE (SALVIA OFFICINALIS)

GROWING Grow sage in full sun in a rich, perfectly drained clay loam. Plants prefer a fairly neutral soil, pH 6.0 to 8.0. As clay soils often tend to be acid try the following preparation. Dig and break up the soil and throw it into a ridge 15 to 20 cm above soil level. Work in 300 g dolomite per square metre and a week to ten days later incorporate a heavy dressing of animal manure. A raised bed which is eventually 20 to 25 cm above ground level will ensure good drainage. Space plants 50 cm apart. Sage will tolerate frosts down to -30°C.

Water in dry weather and keep weeds controlled. But don't overwater. Sage tolerates quite dry conditions and may suffer from mildew if too wet. Growth can be maintained where picking is fairly heavy by side dressings of complete fertiliser or mulches of a mixture of equal parts of animal and poultry manure around the plants. As the plants tend to get too woody after three or four years, it is advisable to start new plants at the end of the second year to have replacements ready.

Sage can be grown from seed which is usually sown direct into the growing position in spring, summer or autumn, or it can be sown in pans, boxes or pots for subsequent transplanting. Cuttings strike readily in garden soil or in pots of coarse sand. Plants can be mound layered in winter. Simply heap up around the plant a mound of sandy soil about 20 to 25 cm high and in spring roots will be found to be emerging from many of the covered stems. These can be detached and planted. Alternatively, old plants can be watered, cut back, lifted and split up, each section being replanted immediately.

HONEY DUCKLING WITH SAGE, POTATO AND ONION STUFFING

2 kg duckling
1 cup (250 ml) water
¼ cup (90 g) honey

Stuffing
2 large old potatoes, peeled
30 g butter
3 large onions, chopped
1½ tablespoons chopped fresh sage leaves or
1½ teaspoons dried sage
salt and freshly ground black pepper

To make Stuffing: cook potatoes in boiling salted water until tender. Drain and mash. Melt butter in a large frying pan and cook onions until very soft, without colouring. Combine onions, potatoes and sage. Season with salt and pepper.

Wipe duck with kitchen paper. Insert stuffing, truss with string and set on a rack in a roasting pan. Pour in water and roast duck for 15 minutes in a 200°C (400°F) oven. Reduce heat to 160°C (325°F) and roast for a further 1 hour. Brush duck with warmed honey 10 minutes before the end of cooking time.

To serve, cut duck into quarters. Serve with the stuffing, and vegetables of your choice.

Serves 4

HONEY DUCKLING WITH SAGE, POTATO AND ONION STUFFING

Savory Calamint

SATUREJA HORTENSIS, SUMMER SAVORY
S. MONTANA, WINTER SAVORY

Summer savory is a tender annual growing to 45 cm with narrow bronze-green leaves to 2 cm long and small white or pale lavender flowers.

It is sweeter than winter savory and widely used as a condiment with meats and vegetables, particularly beans, peas and potatoes where it can be used in place of mint and as a substitute for salt in cooking. Medical uses are listed.

Winter savory is a hardy perennial, a small woody sub-shrub, growing usually to about 30 cm but sometimes up to 60 cm. It has small white, lavender or pink flowers.

The narrow, spicy leaves are 2 to 3 cm long and are used like those of summer savory and also for flavouring some liqueurs. It has some medicinal uses. It is an attractive small shrub.

GROWING Both the savories like full sun and a well-drained soil is necessary to both. Summer savory prefers a moderately rich loam, but winter savory is better suited to a light, sandy soil. Both like a fairly neutral soil, pH 6.0 to 7.0. Dressings of ground limestone or dolomite, about 200 g per square metre, should be applied where soils are acid.

Summer savory is grown only in the warm spring-summer season, but winter savory can tolerate frosts to -12°C, although in colder weather it will die back to the roots. It will recover in spring unless the winter is extreme.

Summer savory can be treated like other annual plants. Suppress weeds, water and

apply a liquid manure such as Thrive to maintain growth.

Winter savory needs pruning each spring and light clipping during flowering.

Summer savory is sown in spring when frost danger is over. Sow seeds where they are to grow and then to 45 cm apart.

Winter savory is usually grown from heeled side cuttings or division, because seeds are slow to germinate.

Scented Pelargonium

PELARGONIUM ODORATISSIMUM, APPLE GERANIUM;
P. SCABRUM, APRICOT OR STRAWBERRY GERANIUM;
P. X CITROSUM, ORANGE GERANIUM;
P. CRISPUM, LEMON GERANIUM;
P. X NERVOSUM, LIME GERANIUM;
P. X FRAGRANS, NUTMEG GERANIUM;
P. TOMENTOSUM, PEPPERMINT OR HERB-SCENTED GERANIUM;
P. CAPITATUM, ROSE-SCENTED GERANIUM;
P. GRAVEOLENS, ROSE OR SWEET-SCENTED GERANIUM

Beautiful cultivars are available of some of the scented pelargoniums or geraniums. There are numerous species, some given invalid botanical names in popular listings. The leaf-fragrant pelargoniums are succulent, soft-wooded herbs, becoming woody as they age. The leaves are mostly mid-green and vary in shape from rounded, scalloped or trefoil-shaped leaves, to deeply cut and lacy, fern-like leaves. The flowers are usually small but sometimes attractive. The fragrance of the leaves, especially when rubbed, is the most attractive feature.

Some of the species are used as substitutes for other perfumes, for example, roses. The leaves are used to flavour drinks, jellies and cakes and can be made into herb teas. Some species have medicinal uses.

GROWING While full sun is often recommended, I have grown some of the species, for example, *Pelargonium crispum,* in a quite shady position. Overcrowding should be avoided as this may encourage the spread of rust. An average well-drained soil is best. Drainage is most important. Organic matter such as leafmould, ripe compost or old, cool animal manure can be incorporated in the first digging. Pelargoniums do best with a range of pH 6.0 to 8.0, so acid soils will need some ground limestone or dolomite, at 200 g or more per square metre. Most species will stand a few degrees of frost down to -7°C. Trim back plants from time to time to keep them reasonably compact, as they have a tendency to become straggling.

As seeds may not come true to type, 15 cm cuttings are used. Allow to dry for an hour or two before planting. Half-length cuttings can be taken of dwarfer varieties. Cuttings are firmly planted in pots of coarse sand. Water to keep soil damp but not wet.

ROSE GERANIUM
(PELARGONIUM GRAVEOLENS)

ROSE GERANIUM SORBET

185 g sugar
2 ½ cups (625 ml) water
6 lemons
4 (6 if small) rose geranium leaves,
crumpled
1 egg white
extra leaves, for decoration

Place sugar in a medium-sized saucepan with water. Grate over lemon rind. Heat over low heat and when sugar has dissolved, bring to the boil. Add crushed leaves. Boil for 6 minutes; cool.

Squeeze juice from the lemons and strain into cooled syrup. Pour mixture into cold freezer trays or a metal bowl. Place in a freezer until mixture just begins to freeze. Remove, turn into a bowl and discard geranium leaves. Beat with a whisk until smooth, but not melted. Beat egg white until stiff but not dry, fold lightly through mixture and return to tray. Cover and freeze until firm.

Pile sorbet into chilled glasses and serve decorated with a rose geranium flower and leaves.

Serves 2 to 4

ROSE GERANIUM SORBET

Shallot

ALLIUM CEPA, VARIETY OF THE AGGREGATUM GROUP, SYN. A. ASCALONICUM

These small, generally sterile onions, which multiply by producing small onions around the base, may have as many as fifteen or twenty cloves or segments inside an aggregate skin. They are narrower than the common onion and can grow 30 to 45 cm high. Strictly they are perennials, but are usually treated as annuals. If undisturbed, they may produce occasional flowers in the second year. The usual shallot has a brown skin, but a white-skinned sort is known. It seems to be somewhat stouter in growth than the brown-skinned sort.

The flavour is milder than onions and most agreeable in salads. The green tops are often chopped up for use in salads, omelettes, scrambled eggs and similar dishes or used with tomato or cheese in sandwich fillings.

GROWING Shallots develop their best flavour in full sun and need rich but light, well-drained soil. They are quite gross feeders and should grow in a bed that was manured heavily for a previous crop. Nevertheless, I have grown shallots successfully in beds that were heavily manured just before planting with cow manure that was partially weathered and finely broken. pH 6.0 to 7.0 is desirable, so add lime to acid soils at the rate of 200 to 300 g per square metre. Shallots will stand frost down to -37°C.

Cultivation is mainly weeding and watering when necessary. When planted in well prepared beds subsequent side-dressings are rarely necessary.

Bulbs are lifted when leaves have shrivelled. Dry them out on trays in the sun for a few days and then store for use or for subsequent planting in a cool, dry place. For replanting, separate the cloves and plant with half the bulb below soil level. Water lightly to avoid washing them out before they have made roots. Space 10 to 15 cm apart in rows 25 to 30 cm apart. Plant from April to June in most areas and again in August to September according to the weather.

Sorrel

RUMEX SCUTATUS, FRENCH SORREL;
R. ACETOSA, SOUR DOCK;
R. PATIENTIA, MONK'S RHUBARB, PATIENCE

The sorrels are weedy, hardy, perennial herbs. They have many common names. French sorrel has prostrate or upright stems, large heart-shaped leaves and may reach 50 to 60 cm. Sour dock or garden sorrel grows 80 to 90 cm, and has arrowhead shaped leaves. Monk's rhubarb can reach 180 cm and has large leaves to 30 cm long.

Culinary uses are rare today except by dedicated herb users, and in some countries such as Egypt or France. Young leaves can be finely chopped in potato salad, or a lettuce or mixed salad and will add a refreshing sharp acid taste. There are other culinary uses. Children still sometimes chew the leaves because of their pleasing acid taste. Some medicinal uses are listed.

GROWING Sorrels grow easily in almost any position and any reasonable soil, but full sun suits them. For best leafage a rich, well manured soil, as for cabbage, rhubarb or lettuce, should be provided, pH 6.0 to 7.0, just below or at neutral point. Lime should be applied to acid soils, using 100 to 200 g of ground limestone or dolomite. Frost protection except in extreme cold is unnecessary because plants tolerate frosts down to -35°C.

The smaller sorrels can be planted 30 to 45 cm apart and monk's rhubarb, or herb patience as it is sometimes called, 50 to 60 cm apart. Do not allow the plants to dry out or leaves will wilt and tips burn. Keep flowering stalks cut out, unless seed is wanted. Save seed only from the best plants, that is the fastest growing with lush, well-flavoured leaves. Lay baits for snails if they appear.

Propagation is easy from seed which can be broadcast or sown thinly in drills in spring. Thin seedlings to the required distance apart. Thinnings can be transplanted.

Old plants can be dug in spring or autumn and divided. Cut back soft upper tips. Replant and keep watered well until new growth is evident. Remove any leaves that show signs of wilting.

Tansy

TANACETUM VULGARE, GOLDEN BUTTONS

Common tansy is a rather coarse perennial herb with a grooved angular stem growing to about 90 cm or more high. It has attractive dark green, fern-like leaves up to 15 cm long and 10 cm wide. A shorter, more compact variety, *T. vulgare* var. *crispum*, is better as a garden plant. The flowers are like small yellow buttons appearing in flat clusters during summer. It has a pungent somewhat bitter odour.

Although tansy has been used in cooking in the past, large doses are poisonous. In some countries it is still sold for medicinal use, but in the USA it is regarded as a dangerous drug.

GROWING Tansy will grow in almost any soil and position — sun or part shade. Soils can be heavy or light and vary from rich to poor. It seems to have no special preference for a particular soil pH. It will withstand frost down to -35°C.

Because tansy spreads quickly by underground runners it can easily over-run a garden bed unless kept under control. It is best to plant it in an isolated bed or large planter box.

Propagate from divisions of the mature plant, by root cuttings, or side pieces that strike readily in sand.

SORREL (*RUMEX ACETOSA*)

TANSY (*TANACETUM VULGARE*)

Tarragon

**ARTEMISIA DRACUNCULUS,
FRENCH TARRAGON
ARTEMISIA DRACUNCULOIDES,
RUSSIAN OR FALSE TARRAGON**

Tarragon is a bushy rhizomatous perennial growing from 60 to 150 cm high. Stems are erect and either smooth or hairy. The narrow leaves can grow up to 15 cm long and are olive green in colour and sometimes twisted or segmented. Flowerheads are small and green-white, appearing in loose, drooping clusters in summer, but plants seldom flower fully. Russian tarragon is an inferior strain of tarragon and has much less flavour.

Tarragon is used to make tarragon vinegar and is one of the herbs used in *fines herbes*. Bearnaise sauce and other sauces are made with tarragon vinegar. Chopped leaves in small quantities can be added to chicken, fish and salads, but are overpowering if too many are used. Tarragon has been used medicinally, particularly in parts of Europe.

GROWING Full sun is usually considered best but tarragon will grow in part shade. Give tarragon a well-drained, sandy soil enriched with organic matter — compost and/or decomposed animal manure. A range of pH 6.0 to 7.0 or 7.5 would probably be satisfactory. I have grown tarragon successfully in limed beds and would think that acid soils would need lime or dolomite at 100 to 200 g per square metre.

Free drainage is imperative, as roots and rhizomes may rot in cold, wet weather in the dormant season. Protect the roots under straw or a cloche in very cold winter areas; tarragon stands frost to about -23°C.

Seed is rarely available and cuttings are slow, therefore tarragon is usually grown from divisions. Old plants tend to become too woody, and should be lifted and divided every second or third year in spring or autumn.

**FRENCH TARRAGON
(ARTEMISIA
DRACUNCULUS)**

Thyme

**THYMUS VULGARIS, COMMON
THYME
T. HERBA-BARONA, CARAWAY
THYME
T. X CITRIODORUS, LEMON
THYME**

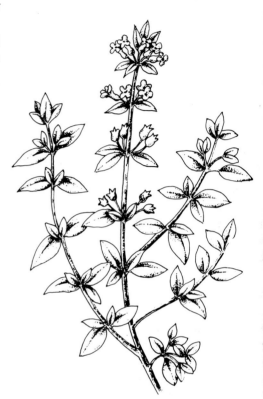

The thymes are all small sub-shrubs, some of them mat-forming and some upright in growth from 20 to 30 cm tall. Those that are listed above are grown for their fragrance. Stems are generally woody at the base and square in cross-section and leaves are fairly small with some sorts having variegated or coloured cultivars or varieties. Flowers mostly appear at the ends of the stems and colours range through pink, red, mauve, purple, lilac and white.

There is confusion in the listings of species, varieties and cultivars of thyme, of which there are many.

Caraway thyme grows to about 12 cm high, with procumbent habit and rose flowers.

Lemon thyme grows to 30 cm high, with lemon-scented broader leaves.

Above ◆ **LEMON THYME (*THYMUS CITRIODORUS*), AND GARDEN THYME (*THYMUS VULGARIS*)**
Right ◆ **CARAWAY THYME (*THYMUS HERBA-BARONA*)**

There is a variegated type.

Thymes are neat little plants and can be used for ground cover, dwarf edgings and small specimen plants.

The thymes are used in *bouquet garni*, in soups, casseroles, and with sage and onions in stuffings. Thyme also has medicinal uses and is processed for its essential oil.

GROWING Give thymes a sunny position, but not too exposed. Thymes prefer a light, dryish, well-drained, even gravelly soil and can be grown in rockeries, crevices in paving or in containers. Acid soils should be limed as thymes prefer a range from pH 6.0-7.0, at or below neutral point. Compost or very old animal manure can be added to the bed, but if thymes receive too rich a bed, for example, with fresh manure they are inclined to grow rank and have inferior flavour. Use dolomite at 100-200 g per square metre when the bed is being prepared. The thymes will stand frosts to -29°C, so need winter protection only in the very coldest areas. Although favouring a fairly dry soil, they do need watering in hot, dry weather.

Thymes can be propagated from seed, which is sown 1 cm deep in shallow drills about 8 to 9 cm apart. Thin plants to 25 to 30 cm apart. Small cuttings will strike in sandy soil or divisions of an old plant will grow readily. Take side pieces which have roots attached.

Turmeric

CURCUMA DOMESTICA SYN. LONGA

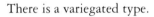

Turmeric is a perennial growing 60 to 90 cm high with tuberous rhizomes of bright orange-yellow flesh and waxy consistency. The canna-like leaves are 45 to 60 cm long, smooth and green, and the flowers are pale yellow and in terminal spikes about 18 cm long.

The rhizomes are ground into a fine, brilliant yellow powder which has an aromatic flavour like ginger. It is used as a constituent of some curries, and as a yellow dye. Seldom used medically, but is used in some chemical tests.

GROWING Turmeric grows best in semi-shade and flourishes in a friable, light but rich, well-drained soil. As the suitable soils are often acid in reaction, lime would be needed only on very acid soils, about pH 5.0 or lower. Turmeric is a suitable plant for growing in the coastal tropics, up to altitudes of 900 metres, and in those areas where temperatures do not fall below 18°C.

Give heavy dressings of organic matter, compost, and animal manure, and water regularly. Use deep mulches in dry weather. Rhizomes are dug when the leaves start to wither. They are then cleaned, boiled and dried before the final processing.

Turmeric is propagated by planting small pieces of rhizome or divisions of the crown. Plant 15 cm deep and space in rows 45 cm apart with 30 cm between plants in the rows.

GROUND TURMERIC

Vanilla

VANILLA PLANIFOLIA SYN. V. FRAGRANS

Vanilla is a large creeping orchid. The mid-green leaves are fleshy, oblong and grow to 20 cm long. Yellow and orange flowers have petals 6 cm long and lip 5 cm long. The aromatic fruits are long seed pods measuring to 20 cm with tiny black, mostly sterile, seeds.

Vanilla is a very popular flavouring used widely in cookery, ice creams, soft drinks, chocolate, and liqueurs. It is also used for perfumes and in scenting tobacco. Its former medical uses have declined.

GROWING Like many orchids, vanilla grows best in light, chequered shade and with protection from strong wind. The soil should be coarse and open. The ideal mixture would comprise ripened compost and chopped osmunda fibre.

Vanilla can only be grown in large glasshouses or the hot, wet tropics; temperatures should not fall below 20°C. Adequate moisture must be provided at all times and strong, low supports. Except in their native habitat, which is tropical America, the flowers must be hand pollinated, hence the need for low supports. Vines are often allowed to climb low-branched trees such as frangipanis and coral trees. Frequent trimming is needed to keep them low.

Vanilla vines are progagated from cuttings 90 to 120 cm long which are planted where they are to grow. A support is chosen, or erected, and one cutting is placed on each side of the support so that the lower ends are just covered with surface soil or growing compost. Alternatively, some growers keep the ends of the cuttings some 2 to 3 cm above the soil level. The cuttings themselves are sprayed with water and roots will grow down into the compost. The above-ground placing minimises loss from rotting. Spacing should be 2 to 2.5 cm between plants.

Violet

VIOLA ODORATA

Violets are small perennial herbs that spread by runners and grow from 10 to 20 cm high. The leaves are rich green, roughly heart-shaped and the fragrant flowers are commonly deep violet blue with varieties in purple, white, pink and pale blue.

Candied violet flowers are used in cake decorations and the fresh flowers are used in salads and sandwich fillings. Violets are used in cosmetics and perfumes.

GROWING Violets need a semi-shaded position, particularly with protection from hot afternoon sun, but can be grown in full sun in cool temperate areas. Soil should be well-drained and enriched with compost and/or manure. Lime should be added to give a soil pH of 6.0 to 7.5. Dolomite or ground limestone can be added at the rate of 150 to 300 g per square metre in acid soils. Plenty

Right ◆ **SWEET VIOLETS (*VIOLA ODORATA*)**
Below ◆ **VANILLA PODS COME FROM A CLIMBING POD WHICH FLOURISHES IN THE WET TROPICS**

of moisture is needed and watering must be regular in dry weather. Violets are hardy and tolerate frosts to -29°C.

The plants are easy to propagate from division of the old plants in autumn. For best results divide at least every second year and space plants 25 to 30 cm apart.

SWEET VIOLETS AND WILD STRAWBERRIES

1 bunch sweet violets
1 punnet (250 g) strawberries or alpine strawberries
1 punnet (250 g) blueberries
1 tablespoon caster sugar
1 tablespoon lemon juice

Cinnamon Cream
1 cup crème fraiche
1 teaspoon cinnamon
1 tablespoon caster sugar
grated rind 1 orange
1 tablespoon orange juice

Remove stems from violets. Rinse strawberries and blueberries. Place in a bowl and fold through caster sugar and lemon juice.

To make Cinnamon Cream: Beat crème fraiche with cinnamon, caster sugar and orange rind. Fold through juice and spoon into a bowl. Chill until required. Serve with Heart-shaped Biscuits.

Serves 4

VIOLET (*VIOLA ODORATA*)

HEART-SHAPED BISCUITS

1 cup (250 g) plain flour, sifted
60 g butter
½ cup (90 g) icing sugar, sifted
2 egg yolks
vanilla icing sugar, to dust

Place flour in a bowl and make a well in the centre. Place butter and sugar in the centre. Rub butter and sugar between the fingertips of one hand until creamy. Add egg yolks and vanilla. Sweep around with your other hand, gathering the flour into the centre. Mix to form a soft dough. Knead very lightly, wrap plastic wrap and chill for 10 minutes.

Roll dough out on a lightly floured surface until very thin. Using a 5½ cm heart-shaped cutter, cut out hearts, set on a baking tray. Bake in a 190°C (375°F) oven for 12 minutes or until biscuits are pale gold. Cool on a wire rack. Dust with icing sugar. Store in an air-tight tin.

Makes 24

Woodruff

GALIUM ODORATUM SYN. ASPERULA ODORATAZ

Woodruff is a low-growing perennial herb that spreads rapidly. The aromatic leaves grow in whorls of 6 to 8 leaves every 4 to 5 cm along the stems which may be from 15 to 30 cm high. Each leaf is narrow, about 4 cm long and tipped with a bristle. Flowers are small, white, and in loose clusters.

Woodruff makes a useful ground cover in shady parts of a herb garden. The leaves are used to flavour wine and wine cups or for a tea, and have also been used medicinally.

GROWING Woodruff needs shade or semi-shade and grows well in woodland conditions. The soil should be well-drained, moist and enriched with compost or animal manure. Lime would be necessary only in strongly acid soil. Woodruff is hardy and tolerates temperatures to -29°C.

Plants can be divided in spring or autumn and planted 20 to 30 cm apart. Seed is used but unless fresh is very slow to germinate.

Wormwood

ARTEMISIA ABSINTHIUM, COMMON WORMWOOD, ABSINTHE

Wormwood is a coarse perennial herb growing from 45 or 50 cm up to as much as 120 cm high. The stems are erect with dissected silvery-grey leaves, but the lower, more woody stems may be brown. The clusters of small green-yellow flowers grow in the leaf junctions.

Wormwood is bitter and aromatic to taste and has been used in beer-making, absinthe and other drinks, but is rarely used in the kitchen. In concentration, it is a poisonous drug. Medicinal uses are still listed. Sachets of wormwood leaves in clothes closets are said to repel moths. Wormwood is also grown for its ornamental leaves and for useful, small hedges. Plants do well in areas close to the sea where other plants may burn.

GROWING Wormwood does best in full sun and needs a well-drained soil such as a light, sandy loam that is not over-rich in organic matter, with a range of pH 6.0 to 8.0. Lime should be added to all but alkaline soils, using 300 to 400 g dolomite on acid soils. Wormwood is frost hardy and can stand temperatures to -35°C. Plants should be trimmed back after flowering and also during the growing period if they are becoming too leggy.

WORMWOOD (*ARTEMISIA ABSINTHIUM*)

Propagate by seed, cuttings or division of old plants; all methods are quite easy. Seed germinates readily; 10 cm cuttings of side pieces strike readily in pots in a mixture of 1 part peatmoss to 3 parts of coarse sand.

Yarrow

ACHILLEA MILLEFOLIUM, COMMON YARROW

Named after Achilles, who, according to legend used the plant to treat his wounds. A hardy perennial, useful for borders or rockeries, with deeply serrated foliage, and rounded flower heads of tiny, tightly packed blooms usually rangin from bright yellow to white, but occasionally cerise.

There are several species, with flowers being yellow or white. The common yarrow has round flat heads of white and rose-coloured flowers, which grow to 60 cm high.

Some species are used as flavouring for herbs and curries.

GROWING Achilles will grow in any soill, provided there is reasonable drainage, and although they are sun-loving, will flower quite well in semi-shade. Plants are best divided in autumn or spring and side shoots taken during winter will yield new plants. Most conditions are suitable except hot tropical.

YARROW (ACHILLEA MILLEFOLIUM) TENDS TO NATURALISE IN WET AREAS

Zedoary

CURCUMA PALLIDA SYN. C. ZEDOARIA

Zedoary is a tropical perennial with a tuberous rhizome, similar to turmeric and sometimes mistaken for it. It grows to about 75 cm high. Large, stalked leaves measure from 25 to 60 cm long and 15 cm wide, and are green with a purple or chocolate midrib. Flowers are yellow with white calyx in spikes from 10 to 15 cm long.

The tubers yield a starch similar to arrowroot and a flavour somewhat like ginger. Zedoary is used as a spice and in curries, and has some medicinal uses.

GROWING Zedoary is grown in partial shade and needs a rich, well-drained, open soil. A sandy loam to which heavy dressings of old animal manure are added is suitable. Lime is required only on soils that are strongly acid, dolomite at 200 g per square metre could be applied. Side dressings of manure or a mulch of manure can be given in the hottest season. Drench with water in dry spells.

Propagate by dividing the rhizomes and plant in rows 45 cm apart each way.

AN INDOOR HERB GARDEN SURROUNDED BY FLOWERS

Controlling Pests and Diseases

Most of the herbs listed in this book are not particularly susceptible to the common pests and diseases that attack garden plants. Their comparative immunity may result partly from the strong aromas in their tissues, but other factors must be involved because some strongly aromatic herbs are attacked by pests and are susceptible to disease.

The mints, which are strongly fragrant, are attacked by grasshoppers and caterpillars. In fact, the mints in my garden seem to attract more grasshoppers than some of the other plants.

SUSCEPTIBLE HERBS

BAY (*Laurus nobilis*) The bay tree seems to be particularly susceptible to pink wax scale. White wax scale can also be a nuisance. The common grasshoppers also seem to be partial to bay leaves.

CHICORY (*Cichorium intybus*) Slugs, snails and some caterpillars attack chicory readily.

CHIVES (*Allium schoenoprasum*) are sometimes infested with aphids or attacked by downy mildew.

ELDER (*Sambucus nigra*) The common European elderberry does not suffer much from pests or diseases, but birds are partial to the berries. However, the golden elderberry suffers from leaf scorch in areas where the summer sun and drying winds affect it. Plant in semi-shade, and mulch heavily to provide a cool root run with adequate moisture, and this will help to avoid disfigurement of the attractive leaves.

MINT (*Mentha species*) Grasshoppers and caterpillars of various kinds attack mint, but rush disease is more serious. Should rush occur, lime the soil and do not replant with mint for some years.

Burn sticks and straw over the bed to kill the spores. Obtain new, clean plants and burn the old ones.

SCENTED PELARGONIUM (*Pelargonium species*) Plants may be affected by rust, characterised by reddish pustules especially on the undersides of the leaves.

SHALLOTS (*Allium cepa, syn. A. ascalonicum*) Aphids and downy mildew occasionally attack shallots.

SORREL (*Rumex species*) Sorrel is susceptible to damage by slugs and snails.

VIOLET (*Viola species*) Aphids congregate under the leaves, damaging plants and discouraging growth.

PEST CONTROL

APHIDS These are small, winged and wingless, soft-bodied sucking insects, black, brown, green or reddish in colour, that congregate on young shoots, young flower buds or the undersides of leaves. They can cause severe damage by sucking sap, which distorts flowers and leaves. More serious still is the risk of transmitting virus diseases to healthy plants.

Spray with soapy water or a spray such as maldison or dimethoate (Rogor). Sometimes it is possible to dislodge small infestations by a fast jet of water from the hose. Early treatment is essential because aphids multiply rapidly.

CATERPILLARS AND GRASSHOPPERS Caterpillars can be controlled safely by using Lane's Dipel which does not harm other living things. Carbaryl sprays control both these pests.

RED SPIDER AND OTHER MITES These move about slowly on the undersides of leaves and are scarcely visible to the naked eye. Control with Kelthane at maker's strength.

SOIL NEMATODES These are controlled by soil dressings such as Nemacur used before planting.

THRIPS These are small, dark, narrow, flying insects only 1 mm long that do much damage to flowers. Use Rogor at maker's recommended strength.

SCALE PESTS Spray with white oil in mid-November and December following carefully the maker's mixing instructions. Usually two sprays will be necessary.

SLUGS AND SNAILS These are easily controlled by using the pelleted slug and snail baits. Use at intervals until the pests are gone.

BUGS AND BEETLES These include sucking and leaf-eating pests which can generally be controlled with carbaryl.

CUTWORMS These are fat, dirty-looking greyish caterpillars that lurk in the soil during the day. They often chew off young plants just above the soil, and the damage is sometimes mistaken for damping-off. A soil fumigant such as Disyston 5 will control them. Pyrethrum and derris dusts and sprays are among the safest to use and give quite good protection.

DAMPING-OFF This is a serious disease in young seedlings which may cause the loss of a complete crop. It is caused by a soil-borne organism, so that one way of preventing it is to use

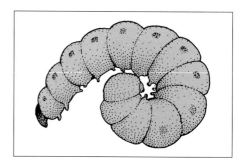

CUTWORM

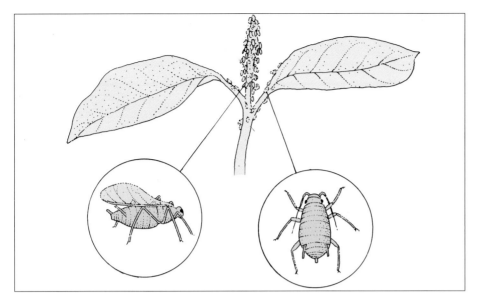

APHIDS

sterilised seed compost and sterilised seed trays or boxes. The former can be bought in packs at garden stores. Sterilise boxes and trays by boiling for a minute or two before using.

Damping-off appears as a shrivelling of the seedling stem near soil level. The plant topples over and dies. If an attack has started, drench the remaining plants and the soil or compost with a solution of Captan at the maker's recommended strength, which is usually at 6 g Captan to 5 litres water.

POWDERY MILDEW This affects leaves, flowers and buds and appears as a grey to white powdering on the surface. This is often more prevalent in humid weather. Spray with Benlate using a 2-gram sachet to 5 litres of water.

RUST Appearing on the leaves as reddish or brown spots or pustules, rust occurs mainly on the undersides of the leaves with only a small yellowish spot showing on the upper surface. To control rust, spray with Dithane (mancozeb), 8 g in 5 litres of water or with zineb at 10 g to 5 litres of water. Each of these sprays should first be mixed with a small quantity of water to make a thin cream, which is stirred into the required quantity of water.

DOWNY MILDEW Leaves tend to be pale in colour, then go yellow and shrivel. The surface may be faintly grey or powdered with a white mould. Spray with Dithane, zineb or copper oxychloride at the above mentioned rates.

There are serious wilts, rots and virus infections for which no real cure is available. Herbs seem to be fairly free of these, but if any plants wilt or rot, with the plant shrivelling or collapsing, it is best to dig up the plant and burn it to destroy the infectious organisms.

It is always wise to control insect pests to some extent, because sucking insects such as aphids or thrips may transmit serious diseases to otherwise healthy plants.

USING HERBS

Some herbs have many uses, for example, lavender, which is used for low hedges or edgings, perfumery, lavender water, soaps, sachets, face creams, talcum and face powders. It is also used medicinally, and even has culinary uses (recipes for lavender sugar can still be found in some herb books and crystallised lavender flowers can be used in cake decoration). Not many of the herbs are as versatile as lavender, though they each have their uses.

Some herbs are surprisingly ornamental. For example, chives (*Allium schoenoprasum*) might seem as purely utilitarian as the commonplace garden onion but with a slightly less pungent flavour, and yet they make decorative dwarf edging plants and are also very attractive in the flower garden. Their slender, pointed leaves and mauve, pincushion flowers delight the eye and can even be used in small posies.

Perhaps the most essential remark to be made on herbs is the warning that accurate identification of them is necessary. Many herbs, that is, small growing, more or less soft wooded plants, produce lethal poisons. Before using any herb in cooking or salads, be absolutely certain of its identity and make sure that no lethal plant has been grown in the garden in error.

Which herb for what

Angelica	used crystallised in cakes, biscuits, marmalades
Anise	fresh leaves used in salads, steamed vegetables, shellfish; aniseed used in cookies, apple pie
Basil	pesto, tomato dishes, eggs, mushrooms, green salads, pasta
Bay	part of bouquet garni, used in stews, soups, poached fish, marinades; single leaf sometimes used in milk puddings
Bergamot	young leaves good in salads and with pork
Caraway	seeds flavour breads, cakes, biscuits, pasta, cabbage, parsnips, turnips, peas, baked apples
Chervil	part of fines herbes traditionally used with eggs, chicken, fish, salads, soups and sauces; chervil soup is also delicious
Chives	omelettes, salads, soups, mayonnaise, cream cheese
Coriander	seeds indispensable to curries, pickled fruit; whole fresh leaves used with fish, cauliflower, beetroot, celery
Dill	leaves and seeds go well with soups, salads, white sauces, egg dishes, seafood, cheese, pickles and vinegar
Fennel	fresh leaves or seeds taste good in soups, fish, cottage cheese, bread, cakes
Garlic	stews, Italian dishes, omelettes, lamb, vegetables
Ginger	curries, pickles, chutneys, vegetables, Chinese cooking, cakes and biscuits
Horseradish	shellfish, poultry, pork, beef
Hyssop	rabbit, lamb, salads, vegetables, drinks, stewed peaches, apricots
Lemon balm	summer drinks, salads, pork, lamb, chicken stuffings
Lemon verbena	fruit salads, punches, summer drinks
Lemon grass	Thai cooking, curries, salads
Lovage	soups, stews, salads, sauces
Marjoram	Italian dishes, tomatoes, pumpkin, potatoes, meat, chicken and rice
Mint	lamb, young vegetables, fruit salad and cool summer drinks
Nasturtium	salads, sandwiches, cream cheese
Oregano	see Marjoram
Parsley	part of bouquet garni used in stews and meat dishes; fresh leaves go with almost anything — salads, fish soups, vegetables, stews
Sage	stuffings, meat, salads, soups, cold drinks
Salad burnet	salads, fruit, fruity cups and summer drinks
Savory	sauces, drinks, vegetables e.g. peas, beans, squash
Sorrel	salads, soups, sauces, vegetable purees
Tarragon	chicken, fish, vegetables
Thyme	essential for bouquet garni used in casseroles and meat dishes; also goes well with zucchinis, tomatoes

**FISH BARBECUED
WITH FENNEL**

curly-leaved parsley

basil

sage

flat-leaved parsley

coriander

thyme

bush basil

lemon
thyme

rosemary

variegated
thyme

dill

garlic
chives

marjoram

chives

oregano

mint

tarragon

Herbs Year Round

In the best of all possible worlds, you would use fresh herbs all year round, but many herbs are annuals and even perennials often die back in winter, so we have to make do with dried ones. If a recipe stipulates a quantity of fresh herbs, you can always replace it with one-third to one-quarter the amount of dried.

Although dried herbs lose some natural oils and vitamins, they still retain much of their flavour if correctly dried, and they are indispensable when the garden is bare. Dried herbs do eventually lose their flavour and become stale, however, so if you have jars of dried herbs over a year old, throw them out and start again. Store all your herbs in small, glass, airtight containers and never position the herb rack near a heat source, such as the stove, as the herbs will lose their flavour even faster.

HARVESTING

Wait until the new leaves or flower buds are beginning to unfurl. Pick your herbs immediately after the morning sun has evaporated the dew but before the heat of the day has begun. Herbs are at their most potent then. Never harvest herbs in wet or humid conditions.

The time of year for harvesting, as a general rule, is any time when the leaves, flowers, seeds or roots (depending on which part you are wanting) are well advanced but still young and fresh. Seeds must be collected from the old flower heads when they are mature (often they are brown and brittle).

DRYING

Dry herbs on racks, slats or simply hang them upside down by their stems in a dry, cool place with good air circulation. You can use flyscreen frames or make your own by stretching muslin or hessian over an old picture frame. The important thing is that the air should reach every part of the plant. Lay the herbs out so they have plenty of space and turn them every few days. Never put them in the sun as this robs them of their colour, fragrance and valuable properties.

If you are gathering them into bunches, keep these small and as loose as possible, so that herbs in the middle of the bunch dry as well as those on the outside. When the leaves or flowers are so dry they become crackly, strip them from their stalks and store them. Label the jar with its name and date.

A good short cut is to use your microwave oven. Lay out fresh herbs on absorbent paper, place in the oven, and cook on LOW for 3 minutes.

To collect seeds from herbs, such as dill, fennel and caraway, cut stalks carrying flower heads, place them in a paper bag head-first and secure with a rubber band tied around the top. Rub the stalk heads by hand through the paper bag.

For herbs which are valued for their roots, such as horseradish, valerian and dandelion, dig up the roots and wash them thoroughly, removing any hairs or unappetising parts. Cut roots lengthways into 1 cm wide strips and lay them out, on your herb drying racks or in the oven, on a very low heat with the door slightly ajar. Keep a close eye on them in the oven or they may burn. To test for dryness, try snapping the lengths in half — if they bend but refuse to break, they need more drying. When dry, store the roots in tissue paper in an airtight, labelled jar. Grate the roots as required

FREEZING

Some herbs, like parsley and chives, are better frozen than dried. Pick only the strong young leaves. Wash and chop them, then wrap them in aluminium foil and label. Make up parcels small enough for a single meal, so you don't need to open them more than once. These should keep for two months. For longer-term storage, blanch before freezing.

HANG BUNDLES OF HERBS UPSIDE DOWN TO DRY

Herbs in the Kitchen

BOUQUET GARNI

Bouquet garni is a small package of basic herbs, tied up in a cheesecloth bundle and dangled over the edge of casseroles and hotpots to give flavour to stews, soups and other 'wet' dishes. The three classic herbs are: parsley, bay leaf and thyme but sage, marjoram and rosemary are always a welcome addition and you can experiment with other herbs. Bouquets garni are often added to a dish with a few peppercorns, a small carrot and a stalk of celery.

BASIC RECIPE

1 bay leaf
2 sprigs fresh parsley
1 sprig fresh thyme

Collect the herbs, dry and chop them. Mix together and put a little onto a square, 12 cm x 12 cm, of muslin or cheesecloth and gather up the corners. Tie up the bundle of herbs with a piece of string long enough to drop into the pot, leaving enough string over the edge for pulling out after cooking. A collection of half a dozen bouquets garni, packed neatly into a box, could make an ideal gift for a gourmet.

FINES HERBES

Sometimes in a recipe you will come across the term fines herbes. These are a mixture of chervil, chives, parsley, tarragon and occasionally lemon thyme, in equal proportions. If you grow these herbs in your garden, an airtight jar of fines herbes would make a beautiful gift for someone who loves cooking. They can be used fresh or dried but for the purposes of a gift, dried are more suitable. Parsley and chervil dry best in a warm oven while the other herbs can be dried in small bunches hung in the air. Chop the leaves and small stalks of the dried herbs finely. Mix them together well and fill an airtight pot or jar. Label and decorate with a ribbon. Fines herbes are traditionally used in egg, chicken and fish dishes, in salads, soups, sauces and even sandwiches. They are also delicious with lightly cooked vegetables.

Equipment

Necessary equipment can be as simple as a chopping board and a small sharp knife. Some recipes call for you to lightly 'bruise' fresh herbs. This is most easily done in a mortar and pestle, preferably made of marble or earthenware. Bruising herbs with the pestle releases their flavours quickly.

PARSLEY, THYME, BAY LEAVES AND PEPPERCORNS MAKE THE CLASSIC BOUQUET GARNI

Mayonnaise and Dressings

SAUCE BEARNAISE

This sauce goes well with grilled steaks, fish or chicken. It is a beautifully rich sauce so serve it sparingly.

⅓ cup (80 ml) white vine vinegar
2 shallots, chopped
1 bay leaf
few peppercorns
1 tablespoon dried tarragon
3 egg yolks
pinch salt
185 g unsalted butter
1 teaspoon chopped fresh tarragon

Place vinegar, shallots, bay leaf, peppercorns and dried tarragon in a smalll saucepan. Bring to the boil. Simmer to reduce liquid to 1 tablespoon. Strain and cool.

Place egg yolks, reduced cooled vinegar and salt in a food processor and blend. Melt butter until foaming. With the motor running, add sizzling butter in a slow steady stream. Add fresh tarragon and season to taste. Serve warm.

Note: If sauce is to be reheated or kept warm, set the bowl in a small pan of hot water, stirring frequently.

Makes about 1 cup (250 ml)

PESTO MAYONNAISE

PESTO MAYONNAISE

Serve as a dressing over pasta salad or as an accompaniment to cold meats, Vary the consistency by adding a little water to the finished dressing, depending on how you are going to use the mayonnaise.

3 egg yolks
1 tablespoon Dijon-style mustard
1 tablespoon white wine vinegar
3 cloves garlic
1½ cups (375 ml) olive oil
salt and freshly ground pepper
9 tablespoons fresh basil leaves
3 tablespoons fresh parsley leaves
3 tablespoons grated Parmesan

Blend egg yolks, mustard, vinegar and garlic in a food processor, until smooth. With motor running, add oil in a slow steady stream until a thick mayonnaise has formed. Season to taste with salt and pepper. Add basil and parsley, blend until smooth. Blend in Parmesan. Add water if the mayonnaise is too thick.

Makes 2 cups (500 ml)

TZATZIKI DRESSING

1 medium-sized green cucumber
2 cloves garlic, crushed with salt
1½ cups (375 ml) plain yoghurt
freshly ground black pepper
1 tablespoon chopped fresh mint

Peel cucumber, halve and scoop out seeds. Grate cucumber finely into a bowl. Drain some of the cucumber liquid. Add garlic and yoghurt. Beat with a wooden spoon until puréed. Season with black pepper and stir through chopped mint.

Makes 2 cups (500 ml)

AIOLI

12 to 16 cloves garlic, coarsely chopped
3 egg yolks
salt and freshly ground pepper
2 cups (500 ml) olive oil
juice 2 lemons

Purée garlic and egg yolks in a food processor. Add salt and pepper. With motor still running, add oil in a thin stream, slowly at first. As the sauce thickens, add lemon juice and taste, adding a little more lemon juice, salt or pepper if necessary. This sauce is delicious with seafood.

Makes 2½ cups (625 ml)

Oil and Vinegar

The foundation of a good dressing is the oil and vinegar used. There are a great variety and the ones you choose depend on the type of salad. Choose oils and vinegars to complement each other and use various herbs for an original dressing.

HERB INFUSED OIL

2 cups (500 ml) olive oil
3 tablespoons fresh herbs
extra sprig fresh herb

Warm olive oil and pour into a clean jar with fresh herbs. Cover and leave to steep for two weeks. Strain oil through a fine cheesecloth into a bottle. Add a sprig of fresh herb to each bottle, seal and label. Store in a cool dark place until required.

Makes 2 cups (500 ml)

OIL AND VINEGAR DRESSING

¼ cup (60 ml) white wine vinegar
pinch salt
pinch dry mustard powder
½ cup (125 ml) salad oil
freshly ground black pepper
2 tablespoons chopped fresh parsley or a combination of parsley and tarragon

Beat vinegar in a bowl with salt and mustard powder. Gradually add oil, drop by drop, and season with pepper. Stir in optional herbs and pour dressing over the salad of your choice just before serving.

Makes ¾ cup (180 ml)

LEFT TO RIGHT: RED WINE VINEGAR, HERB INFUSED VINEGAR, CORN OIL, VIRGIN OLIVE OIL, WALNUT OIL, SESAME OIL, GRAPESEED OIL

HERB INFUSED VINEGAR

4 cups (1 litre) wine vinegar
6 tablespoons fresh herbs
extra sprig fresh herb

Combine vinegar with fresh herbs, bruised slightly in a glass or earthenware bowl. Cover and leave to infuse for two weeks. Strain through a double piece of cheesecloth into clean, sterilised bottles. Add a sprig of fresh herb to each bottle, cork and label.

Makes 4 cups (1 litre)

HERB VINAIGRETTE

To make ⅓ cup (80 ml):
1 tablespoon Dijon-style mustard
1 tablespoon white wine vinegar
1 tablespoon chopped fresh herbs, such as chives, parsley, marjoram, thyme or mint
4 tablespoons olive oil
salt and freshly ground black pepper

To make 1 cup (250 ml):
2 tablespoons Dijon-style mustard
3 tablespoons white wine vinegar
3 tablespoons chopped fresh herbs, such as chives, parsley, marjoram, thyme or mint
¾ cup (180 ml) olive oil
salt and freshly ground black pepper

Place mustard in a bowl and whisk in vinegar and herbs. Gradually whisk in oil until mixture thickens. Season with salt and freshly ground pepper.

This dressing may be made and stored in the refrigerator until required. Add fresh herbs just before serving if liked. A split clove of two or garlic may also be added.

Note: Varying the type of oil or vinegar, or adding lemon juice, will give you a different dressing every time. Also, the flavour will change dramatically every time you vary the herbs.

Herb Bread and Butter

Herb breads have been enjoyed for centuries. For those who like baking their own bread, simply add a pinch of your favourite dried herbs to a basic bread recipe.

Herb butters are an invaluable part of cooking, used to flavour a variety of dishes. Maitre d'hotel, a famous butter made with butter, lemon juice and parsley, is used for grilled fish, grilled chicken and pan-fried veal escalopes.

Rosemary Butter goes beautifully with loin of lamb or can be used to add flavour to steamed vegetables accompanying a lamb or veal dish. And of course herb butters in any shape or form are ideal to flavour a French breadstick to make herb bread. Herb butters may be frozen for up to three months if well wrapped in a double layer of freezer wrap or aluminium foil.

Garlic, or Anchovy and Herb Butters are delicious with barbecued meat, but you can use them with whatever you like. A chilled dish of herb butter makes a wonderful addition to a simple meal.

HERB BREAD

1 small French breadstick
125 g favourite herb butter

Cut bread into diagonal slices, keeping the loaf intact by leaving the base of each slice attached.

Make the herb butter according to the directions given in the recipe, keeping the butter softened. Spread thickly on both sides of each slice of bread. Wrap loaf in a large sheet of foil.

Place in a preheated 200°C (400°F) oven for 10 minutes or until the butter has melted. Open the foil parcel a few minutes before the end of cooking time to crispen the loaf if liked.
Serve hot.

HERB BREADS AND A SELECTION OF HERB BUTTERS

ANCHOVY AND HERB BUTTER

250 g butter
5 anchovy fillets
6 tablespoons finely chopped mixed herbs, such as parsley, chives,
basil, chervil or marjoram
freshly ground black pepper
grated rind and juice ½ lemon

Cream butter in a bowl until softened. Drain oil from anchovy fillets and mash until smooth, using the back of a fork. Fold through butter with herbs, black pepper, lemon rind and juice. Spoon onto a piece of plastic wrap, freezer film or aluminium foil. Form into a log shape and chill or freeze until required. Use to flavour barbecue steak both during cooking and as an accompaniment.

Makes 1 cup (250 g)

CHIVE BUTTER

125 g butter
2 teaspoons lemon juice
½ bunch chives, snipped
1 teaspoon grated lemon rind

Cream butter until softened. Beat in lemon juice. Fold through chives and lemon rind. Spoon butter onto a piece of plastic wrap, freezer wrap or aluminium foil. Form into a long shape and chill until firm. Cut off and use as required. Fresh herb butters may be frozen for up to three months.

Makes ½ cup (125 g)

ROSEMARY BUTTER

125 g butter
2 teaspoons rosemary spears
freshly ground black pepper
2 teaspoons lemon juice
1 teaspoon Dijon-style mustard

Cream butter in a bowl and fold through rosemary. Season with black pepper, lemon juice and mustard. Spoon onto a sheet of plastic wrap, freezer film or aluminium foil. For into a log shape and chill or freeze until required.

Makes ½ cup (125 g)

GARLIC AND HERB BUTTER

250 g butter
4 to 5 cloves garlic, crushed with salt
3 tablespoons chopped, mixed fresh herbs such as parsley, chives,
marjoram, oregano or rosemary
2 tablespoons chopped shallots

Cream butter in a bowl until softened. Stir through crushed garlic, mixed herbs and shallots. Spoon butter onto a piece of plastic wrap, freezer wrap or aluminium foil. Form into a log shape and chill until firm. Cut off and use as required.

Alternatively, place butter in a small pot and use while cooking barbecued meats. Use to butter a French breadstick for herb and garlic bread

Makes 1 cup (250 g)

TARRAGON BUTTER

A very delicately flavoured butter. Use with chicken while roasting
or spread a dob of butter on steamed vegetables.
125 g unsalted butter
1½ tablespoons chopped fresh tarragon or 1½ teaspoons dried
2 teaspoons lemon juice

Cream butter until softened in a bowl. Stir through tarragon and lemon juice. Spoon onto a piece of plastic wrap, freezer wrap or aluminium foil and form into a log shape. Chill until ready to use

Makes ½ cup (125 g)

Fresh Fragrance

SACHETS

Fragrant herbal sachets can be hung in wardrobes, placed in chests of drawers or hung in the airing cupboard. They make everything around them smell delicious and are excellent, inexpensive and thoughtful gifts. Add a little dried lemon or orange peel to the sachet to help it retain its perfume.

To make a sachet, cut two pieces of pretty cotton fabric into rectangles 20 cm x 11 cm. Turn right sides together and sew up, 1½ cm from the outside edge, down one long side, across the bottom and up the second side, leaving 2 cm unsewn at the top. Turn down ½ cm from the top, press, then turn down a further 1½ cm. Hand sew this edge down. Attach a small safety pin to the end of a 30 cm length of coloured ribbon and insert it through the casing. Pull the thread through the casing with the safety pin until it emerges at the other end. Turn the bag inside out. Now fill it with crumbled, dried herbs.

The following herbs are all suitable candidates for sachets: angelica, anise, basil, caraway, coriander, scented geraniums, lavender, lemon thyme, lemon verbena, mint, pot marjoram, rose, rosemary, thyme and violet.

MOTH BAGS

Certain herbs are known to repel moths, among them mint, rosemary, sage, southernwood, sweet basil and tansy. To protect winter woollies, make little drawstring herb bags, filled with crumbled dried herbs, and hang them on the hangers of clothes needing moth protection. Cover the garment with a polythene bag or keep the herb bags tucked among moth-prone jumpers.

POTPOURRI

This is a wonderful way of keeping all the rooms in your house smelling fresh and fragrant. Each room can smell different. There is nothing so sweet as catching a drift of perfume from bowls of potpourri. Place them on tables beside sofas or beds for the most noticeable aroma.

Potpourri is a fragrant mixture of flower petals, herbs, ground spices, seeds and barks, preserved with a fixative that both blends the different fragrances and slows down the release of the flowers' natural oils. To enhance the aroma, add a little concentrated oil or essence, available from chemists, to the mixture but don't get too carried away.

There are two ways of making potpourri. The more traditional method is a wet preparation, using only partially dried flower petals, while the more decorative and popular method today is dry preparation.

Suitable flower petals for the basis of a potpourri are: roses, lavender, philadelphus (mock orange), violets, lily of the valley, red bergamot and white jasmine. Suitable fragrant herbs are sage, bay, lemon balm, eau-de-cologne mint, peppermint, bergamot, rosemary and lemon verbena. Spice favourites include cinnamon sticks, ground cloves and ground coriander seeds. Use flowers and buds other than those with a scent, if they dry well, to add colour and bulk to the collection: use marigolds, pansies, cornflowers, hyssop, borage, wattle, bougainvillea and nasturtiums. Add dried orange and lemon peel for a refreshing aroma. Cut only the best peel, avoiding any pith. Dry on paper in a warm oven and store in a dry, dark place until ready for use.

Three fixatives are suitable for potpourri — gum of benzoin, orris root powder and salt. The first two of these are available from chemists.

WET POTPOURRI

Place a layer of partially dried flowers in the bottom of an earthenware crock. Sprinkle a layer of salt on top. Add another layer of flowers and another layer of salt. Continue in this way to the top of the pot. Cover and leave in a cool, airy place for a couple of weeks. Mix in the fragrant dried herbs with a wooden spoon. Seal and leave for another six weeks. Then add a few drops of oil or essence and leave, sealed, for a further two weeks. The preparation is then ready to be spooned into containers.

DRY POTPOURRI

Collect the flower petals in the early morning, after the dew has dried but before the full sun has robbed them of their essential oils. Lay each petal or flower head out separately on paper in a cool, airy place to dry. Don't let the flowers touch or they will stick together. Only when they are completely dried are they ready for the potpourri. To collect enough fragrant flowers, you will have to build up quite a collection. Pick and dry a few each fine day and store in an airtight container until you have enough to make a potpourri.

ROSE POTPOURRI

3 cups rose petals
1 cup lavender or violet flowers
1 cup rose geranium leaves
1 cup mixed dried flower heads and buds
1/2 cup rosemary leaves
2 sticks cinnamon, coarsely ground
20-30 coarsely ground cloves
1 cup fixative
4 drops rose essence

Mix all dry ingredients together. Add drops of essence and mix again. Store the mixture in an airtight container for six weeks. Tip out into small bowls and decorate with colourful dried petals or flowers.

A GREAT VARIETY OF HERBS AND FLOWERS CAN BE INCLUDED IN YOUR POTPOURRI

Fragrant Flavours

Candied and crystallised flowers, petals and leaves have been used for centuries as sweet meats. Exquisitely decorative, they preserve the plant by coating it in sugar which crystallises with repeated boiling and evaporation.

CANDIED AND CRYSTALLISED

What is the difference between candied and crystallised fruits and flowers? Very little. Candied fruits are preserved by boiling with sugar until a thick syrup forms. Crystallised fruits are also boiled with sugar and then rolled in extra sugar to coat with crystals. Blossoms or petals are too delicate to be boiled, so the sugar syrup is poured over them and they are left to set.

CANDIED BLOSSOMS

Sweet flowers such as roses, violets, wattle, honeysuckle, sweet peas and scented geraniums are all edible. They are exquisite when candied and used to decorate a special dessert or cake, or a homemade ice cream or sorbet. Alternatively, offer them in a bowl as a sweet.

3 cups or handfuls edible blooms (weight depends on choice of flower)
2 cups (500 ml) water
3 cups (750 g) granulated sugar

Wash the flowers briefly but very carefully. Remove stems and gently pat dry. Place water and sugar in a heavy-based saucepan and heat slowly to dissolve sugar. Once sugar has dissolved, bring to the boil and boil until small cracks form, 138°C (270°F). Pour about half the syrup into a shallow pan. Let both quantities cool.

Position the flowers on a metal rack inside the pan so that they float on the syrup. Cover with a cloth and leave to stand in a cool place for several hours. Spoon over the remaining syrup to completely cover the flowers. Cover again with a cloth and stand for at least 12 hours in a cool place.

Remove the rack and place it on a tray to drain. Leave until the flowers are completely dry. Store flowers in an airtight container with sheets of baking paper between each flower to prevent them from sticking to each other.

CRYSTALLISED PETALS AND LEAVES

Sugar-coated herb petals and leaves are a beautiful way to preserve herbs. Use to decorate desserts or cakes, or offer as a sweet with coffee.

1 cup edible petals or herb leaves (weight depends on flower chosen)
1 egg white
tiny pinch salt
fine vanilla-spiced or caster sugar

Wash petals or leaves carefully. Pat dry gently with absorbent kitchen paper (do not rinse wattle). Leave flowers whole if very small. Beat egg white with the salt until foamy. Brush it on each petal, flower or leaf with a pastry brush or your fingers. Surfaces should be moist but with no excess egg white.

Shake or dust sugar on both sides. Place gently on a tray lined with baking paper. Dry in the refrigerator for 2 to 3 days. Store in an airtight container in the refrigerator until required.

SCENTED SUGAR

Vanilla sugar is well known and available commercially. It is also easily made by storing a vanilla bean in a jar with caster sugar. Well, what about using scented geranium leaves for a change?

Scented geraniums are among the most fragrant plants in the herb garden. The variety available includes almond, apple, lemon, lime, nutmeg, peppermint and rose geranium. The flavour of these leaves is easily transferred to sugar, by simply layering a handful through a jar of caster sugar. Rose petals, violets, wattle and mints will do the same. Leave the leaves, flowers or petals in the container of sugar and close tightly for a couple of weeks. Use to flavour cakes, biscuits, custards, creams, sorbets, ice cream or even tea.

Left ◆ **CANDYING SWEET PEAS**
Right ◆ **CAKES CAN BE BEAUTIFULLY DECORATED WITH CANDIED AND CRYSTALLISED FLOWERS**

Herbal Teas

These refreshing alternatives are low in tannin and mostly caffeine-free. Whether you choose chamomile tea to get a good night's sleep or fennel to aid your digestion, you can enjoy the refreshing taste of these natural remedies.

Herbal teas are not only curative and soothing, natural tranquillisers which can calm the nervous and digestive systems, they taste good too! If you have a mass of a particular herb growing all over the garden, you will probably have enough leaves or flowers to collect for a good-size packet, tin or box of tea.

They make excellent presents. Pack in attractive containers — remember, lids must be airtight to keep the tea's flavour. Label the tea container and decorate it if you wish. You may like to add some information about the herb tea and what it is used for.

INFUSIONS AND TEAS

Dried or fresh herbs left to steep in boiling water. Many herbal teas have a soothing, refreshing or stimulating effect on the body, and provide a gentle method of treatment which is easy and inexpensive. Most produce excellent flavours, though some are a little bitter. If this is the case, add a little honey to sweeten.

Herbal teas can be drunk hot or cold. Usually the leaves or flowers of the herb are used to make tea but occasionally seeds are used. To extract their goodness, crush seeds with a pestle and mortar before use.

Preparing a herbal tea is like making any other kind of tea. You can use dried or fresh herbs. If using dried herbs, the usual proportions are: 1 teaspoon to each cup of boiling water. If you are using fresh herbs, use three times the quantity of herb. Fresh herbs should be lightly crushed, chopped, or bruised before putting in the teapot, in order to extract their therapeutic properties. A china teapot is most suitable and aluminium should be avoided. Leave the infusion to steep for 5 to 6 minutes. Many herbal teas become bitter if left to steep too long.

Tea Tips

Fennel tea with its aniseed flavour is used to
stimulate the appetite and improve digestion.
Lemon balm leaves make a deliciously fragrant tea
which soothes and calms.
Sage is a popular gargle and has long been
used to soothe sore throats.

Herbal Preparations

These practical preparations, all quite simple and requiring no special equipment, encourage herbs to release their medicinl properties. They make interesting, effective alternatives to chemicals, and are useful for minor ailments.

TINCTURES

A preparation of herbs in alcohol. Rubbing alcohol or voddka is normally used. The usual proportions are 40 g crushed or powdered herb to 600 ml alcohol. Put the two ingredients together in an airtight jar, filled to the top, leave in a warm place and shake the container everyday for 3 to 4 weeks. The tincture is then ready for use. Tincture have a long shelf life and are therefore more useful than decoctions, which only last a short while.

OILS

Another way to encourage herbs to release their properties, by steeping them in oil. Take a jar of vegetable oil and fill it with crushed herbs. Leave it in a sunny or warm place and shake it each day for a couple of weeks. Strain off the herbs and repeat the process with some fresh herbs for another 4 or 5 weeks.

OINTMENTS

Herbs simmered with either lard or petroleum jelly. It is usually simpler to buy these preparations from a health food store.

INHALATIONS

A few drops of essence, dropped into a bowl of steaming water. The idea is to breath in as much of the steam as possible through the mouth and nose. Bend over the bowl with a towel over your head to trap the steam.

POULTICES

A preparation of chopped or crushed herbs wrapped in cheesecloth and applied to a sore spot as hot as you can bear it. Place the herbs in the centre of the piece of cheesecloth, twist it up and tie with string, then dunk the herb bag into a pan of boiling water. Make sure you have the edges of the cheesecloth dry and poking out of the pan, so you can pull it out when the herbs are mushy. Squeeze out any excess moisture and apply immediately to the sore spot. Either

hold it there until it cools or bandage it in position. This treatment draws the poisons out of an infected area, soothes inflammations, and promotes healing.

COMPRESSES

Like a cold poultice. Apply saturated with a cold herbal infusion, to the infected part and remove when it has become warm. Apply another cold, infusion-laden piece of lint and repeat until you feel relief. Compresses are usually used to reduce swellings, such as bruises and black eyes.

DECOCTIONS

The preparation of boiled bark or root of a herb. The bark or root should be washed and then the bark crushed and the roots grated or chopped. The herb is left to simmer, covered in a pan, until the fluid reduces. Sometimes it is left to cool and steep for 12 hours before the liquid is strained off to provide the decoction. This is often a long-winded operation and is not commonly practised in the home these days.

A word of warning

The scientific basis of herbal medicines is still under investigation. Always heed cautionary notes attached to any product or plant description, and never take more than the recommended dosage. Too much of any herb can be dangerous. If you suffer from a medical condition, always check with your doctor or local chemist before taking anything.

It must be remembered that self-help herbal treatments should be used only for mild infections and illnesses. If you are seriously ill, consult your doctor or a professional alternative practitioner, if you prefer.

Finally, if you collect herbs from wasteground or beside motorways and you are absolutely sure whether a herb is what you think it is, get it professionally identified by a botanist or herbalist before going ahead with any treatment. Many plants look like other plants, and it takes time to become proficient at recognising what is what.

Far Left ◆ **A SELECTION OF HERBAL TEAS**

Left ◆ **DANDELION TEA**

Index

Recipe Index